Centre
Stage

ENGLISH AS A SECOND LANGUAGE

Editor
Jeanine Floyd

Proofreader
David Smith

Photo research and permissions
Katie Dickie

Art director
Hélène Cousineau

Graphic design coordinator
Denise Landry

Cover and book design
Sylvie Morissette

Typesetting
Infoscan Collette

Consultants
Mylène St-Cyr, école secondaire L'Escale,
    commission scolaire des Sommets
Dominique Jutras, école secondaire le Carrefour,
    commission scolaire des Patriotes

Illustrations
François Boutet: pages 48, 79, 87, 132
Marie-Andrée Bureau: pages 18, 104, 107, 118–123
Colagène, Jérôme Mireault: pages 28–31, 33, 107, 109–117,
    156–163
Jean Lacombe: pages 16, 17, 64–66, 88, 107, 125–127
Yvan Meunier: pages 59, 60–61 (posters)
Serge Rousseau: pages 107, 129–131

Dépôt légal – Bibliothèque et Archives nationales du Québec, 2006
Dépôt légal – Bibliothèque et Archives Canada, 2006
Imprimé au Canada

ISBN 2-7613-1745-9
123456789 FR 09876
10667 ABCD PLM-12

We'd like to thank our Centre Stage models,
Camille, Catherine, Chantal, Cedric, David, Diane,
Gabriel, Iohahiio, Joshua, Kelly, Martine, Marylyn,
Meagan, Sara-Monique, Stevens and Yasmine, as
well as Cynthia Dufour and her Secondary Cycle One
students at l'École secondaire de la Cité-des-Jeunes.

Photographs

Associated Press: 53, 54(t.r.), 78(b.l.), 101(6)

Bettmann Corbis: page 18(l.e)

© Canadian Museum of Civilization: page 18(l.1.)
    CD2001–296–102,(l.2) CD2001–293–045, (l.4)
    CD2001–282–009,(m.) K2001–2706/CD2001–296–022,
    (r.1) S97–9965/CD2001–272–008,(r.2)
    K2001–2723/CD2001–296–039, 134

Canadian Press: pages 20(4), 35(b. 2), 36(b.), 39(t.r.), 54(b.l., b.r.),
    67, 78(t.l., t.r.), 81(l., m.), 100(8), 101(7)

Dorling Kindersley: pages 3(t), 14(l) Musée Gauguin Tahiti, 14(m),
    18(b. l., m.) PhotoDisc/GettyImages, 19(2), 20(1), 20(2)
    Pearson Learning Group Photo Studio, 35(t. 1) Pearson
    Scott Foresman, 39(b.l.), 56(4, 5, 6), 45 GettyImages, 57(t.r.)
    Pearson Scott Foresman, 57(b.r.) Simon Burdett Ginn
    Needham, 72(5), 73(6, 13), 85(b.l., b.r.), 101(9 b.l., b.r.),
    123(t.), 128(t.) Merril Education, 131(t.) PhotoEdit, 131(b.)
    Prentice Hall School Division,

ERPI photobank: pages 1, 2, 5, 8, 9, 10.l, 12(m. r.), 13, 19(1, 3, 4),
    25–27, 29, 30–34, 35(t.3, t.4, m.1–4, b.1, 4), 37, 40, 41, 45(t.l.,
    t.r., m.l., m.r.,b.l., b.r.), 46(1–3, 6), 47(7, 9, r.), 49, 51(b.), 54(t.l.,
    m.l., m.r.), 55(r.), 56(11), 62(t.1, t.2, b.l.), 63(b.l., b.r.), 68(b.l.,
    t.r.), 69, 74, 76, 77(m.), 93, 97, 100(1–7, 10), 102, 104,
    106(t.1–3, 5), 108–111, 113, 115, 117–122, 124–126,
    128–130, 134–143, 144(l.), 146(t.), 148, 149, 151

Free the Children: page 21

Gilles Potvin: page 70

Musée de la mer, Rimouski: page 71

iStock: pages x, 3(b.) C. Carroll, 6(7.l.) Zack, 12(l.) V. Danilow,
    18(b.r.), 35(t.2) N. Louie, 35(b.3), 39(t.l) T. White, 47(8)
    R. Osborne, 55(l.) G Barskaya, 56(1) R. Wong, 56(2, 3) K.Zirkel,
    56(7) S. Nguyen, 56(8, 9,11), 57(t.l.) S. Moran, 62(b.r.), 62(t.3)
    L. Pettet, 62(t.4) D. Bisogno, 62(l.m.) T. Stajduhar, 63(t.l.)
    A. Rattansi, 63(t.r.), 72(1), 72(2) J. Goodyear, 72(3) R. Smith,
    72(4) D. Philips, 73(1),73(2) T. Hughes, 73(3) D. Hogan, 73(5)
    M. Stay, 73(7) R. Lindberg, 73(8), 73(10) J. Staub, 73(12)
    A. Taylor, 73(14) V. Essen, 73(15) J. Tyler, 92(l.t.) T. Mc, 92(l.m.)
    P. Fairbrother, 92(l.b.) J. Gynane, 92(r.m.) C. Matei, 92(r.b.)
    R. Picard, 96(b.) T. Harrison, 123, 144(r.1) A. Chelnokova,
    144(r.4) G. Barskaya, 146(b.l.), 150

Jupiter Images: pages 6(1, 2.l, 3–7.r, 8), 7(9, 10, 12–16), 14(r.),
    18(t), 20(3), 22(r.), 23(t.), 24(b.), 35(b.3), 36(t.), 56(10), 58,
    62(b.r.), 73(11), 77, 82–84, 85(t.l., t.r.), 87(t.r.), 92(t.l.), 92(t.r.),
    95, 96(t.), 100(9), 101(8), 101(9t.l., t.r.), 105(t.4), 144(r.2, r.3)

Mauricie, Société d'histoire régionale: page 68(b.r.)

Negro Leagues Baseball Museum, Inc.: page 81(r.)

Philip Weltner Library, Oglethorpe University: page 15

Shattuck-St. Mary's School: page 106(b.)

Tango Photographe: photos of the Centre Stage 2 team through-
    out the book

Tiverton Museum of Mid Devon Life, UK: page 17

Centre Stage

ENGLISH AS A SECOND LANGUAGE

Gillian Baxter

Jonathan Munro Jones

Secondary Cycle One
Student's Book 2

ERPi

ÉDITIONS DU RENOUVEAU PÉDAGOGIQUE INC.

5757, RUE CYPIHOT
SAINT-LAURENT (QUÉBEC)
H4S 1R3

TÉLÉPHONE : (514) 334-2690
TÉLÉCOPIEUR : (514) 334-4720
erpidlm@erpi.com

Contents

THE STORIES

THE PROJECTS

THE PORTFOLIO PAUSES 141

Accumulate samples of your work in your portfolio.
Watch your skills improve every time you add something.

THE REFERENCE SECTION

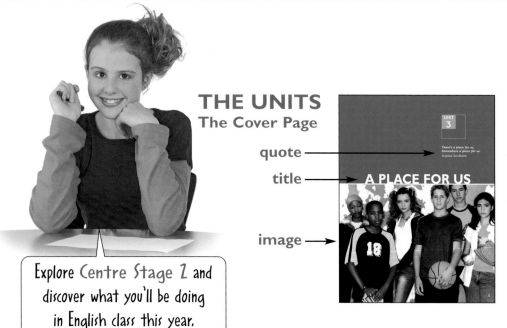

THE UNITS
The Cover Page

quote

title

image

The cover page of the units presents the **title** and an **image** that give you an idea of the theme. It also has a **quote** relating to the theme.

Explore *Centre Stage 2* and discover what you'll be doing in English class this year.

The First Two Pages
These pages help you get ready.

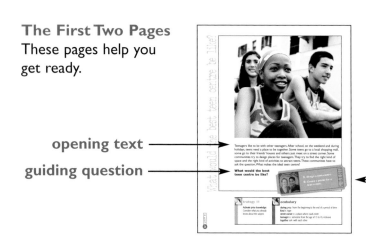

opening text

guiding question

The **opening text** starts you thinking about the topic and theme.

The **guiding question** directs your thinking throughout the unit.

The **Final Curtain ticket** tells you what you will be doing as a final activity.

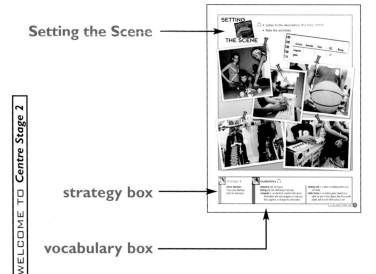

Setting the Scene

strategy box

vocabulary box

The **Setting the Scene** activity starts you on your journey of discovery.

The **vocabulary box** provides definitions of difficult words. A **headset** 🎧 indicates words that you will hear.

The **strategy box** indicates a strategy to use in the activity. All the strategies are explained and illustrated in the Reference Section at the end of the book.

The Activity Pages

number, title

cue card

instruction

notebook

illustration

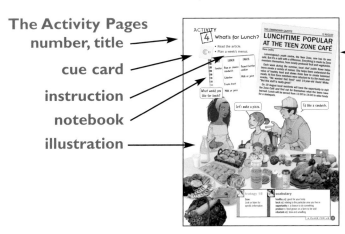

reading texts

The activities expand your knowledge of the theme. They help you build your understanding of English and how to use it.

Each activity starts with a **number** and a **title**.

The **cue card** points you to the functional language you'll need. All the cue cards are explained and illustrated in the Reference Section at the end of the book.

Short **instructions** tell you what to do.

The **notebook** shows you the kind of answer that's expected.

Reading texts give you the chance to practise your reading skills.

Illustrations help you understand what you read and hear.

The **headset** icon indicates a listening activity. These activities help you develop your listening skills.

Speech bubbles provide a model of the kind of interaction you'll take part in.

The **grammar box** explains a key feature of the language used in the text.

headset

speech bubbles

grammar box

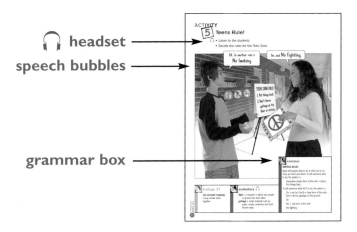

The Final Curtain Activities

In the **Final Curtain** activities, you can use the language, strategies and information you learned in the unit to do something new and different.

The **portfolio icon** reminds you to select the work you want to add to your portfolio.

Introduction to *Centre Stage 2*

The Stories

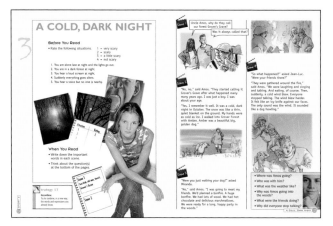

There are four **stories** in *Centre Stage 2*. Not only will they entertain you, but they'll also help you to improve your reading skills.

The Projects

The **projects** allow you to do your own thing. They give you the chance to work on something that interests you and show how much you can do.

The Portfolios

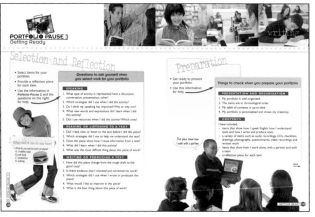

The **portfolio pauses** take you through the steps of creating a portfolio. They help you to put together a collection of significant work.

The AngloFiles give you some interesting and unexpected facts about the English language and the culture of English-speaking countries.

The Reference Section is a learning tool. It can help you learn faster and more easily.

The **strategies** help you to unlock meaning and communicate with others.

The illustrated **cue cards** give you examples of useful expressions.

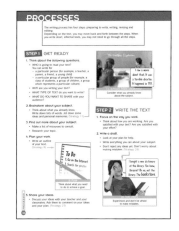

The **processes** tell you how to respond to a text, write a text and produce a media text.

The **focus on form** section lists the grammar features explained in the book and common irregular verbs, and explains some general grammar rules.

The **word list** is your *Centre Stage 2* dictionary. It lists the words defined in the units.

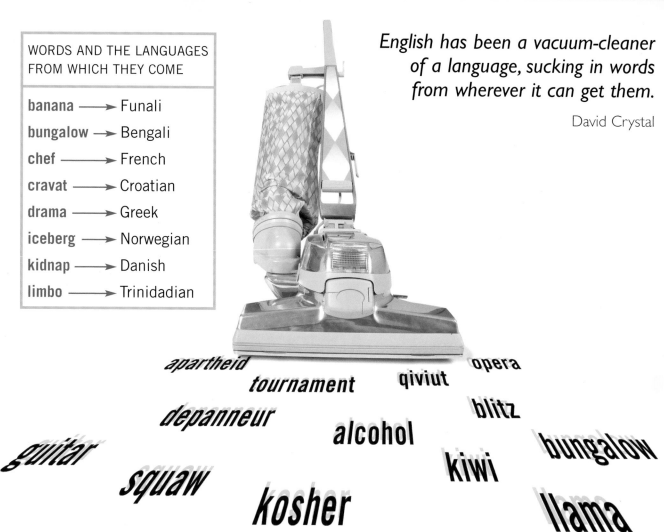

WORDS AND THE LANGUAGES FROM WHICH THEY COME

banana →	Funali
bungalow →	Bengali
chef →	French
cravat →	Croatian
drama →	Greek
iceberg →	Norwegian
kidnap →	Danish
limbo →	Trinidadian

English has been a vacuum-cleaner of a language, sucking in words from wherever it can get them.

David Crystal

apartheid tournament qiviut opera blitz depanneur alcohol kiwi bungalow guitar squaw kosher llama

The history of English is a story of perpetual change. It resulted from invasion, revolution and exploration. The Anglo-Saxons invaded Britain more than 1500 years ago and their language spread across the British Isles. They were farmers and they gave English words like *dog, earth, plough* and *work*. During this time, Christian missionaries came to Britain and introduced words from Latin and Greek, such as *angel, mass* and *psalm*. In 739 CE, the Viking invaders arrived. From their language we have about 900 English words, including *hit, leg, root, skin* and *sky*. The last invasion had the biggest impact on the English language. In 1066, the Norman French conquered England and French became the language of the king, religion, law, science and literature. More than a quarter of English words have their origins in French, from *ambulance, ballet* and *chauffeur* to *version, wardrobe* and *zest*.

As English explorers settled in other parts of the world, they borrowed words from local languages. English-speakers use words from as many as 350 languages. Some of these words, like *pasta* and *judo,* are used around the world, while others, like *depanneur* (convenience store) and *CEGEP* (college) in Quebec and *braaivleis* (barbecue) in South Africa, are just used locally.

English is also a language that will create a new word if none exists. Most of these words arise from advances in technology. They may be new uses for existing words, such as *file* and *server,* or new combinations of words, such as *desktop* (a computer that stands on a desk) and *laptop* (a smaller computer that could be held on one's knees). Others are completely new, such as *blog* and *podcast*.

*Knowing others is intelligence;
knowing yourself is true wisdom.*
Lao Tzu

QUIZ ME!

It's back-to-school time again. Are you ready for some tests or quizzes? Don't worry—these quizzes are just for fun! It's time to get to know your classmates. You might even learn something about yourself.

What do you want to find out about each other?

A. **Create a class Quiz Me! Magazine.**

B. **Design a cover page for Quiz Me! Magazine.**

- Read the information on the magazine cover.
- Find out what's in this issue of *Quiz Me*!

Quiz Me!

Discover that taking tests can be fun!

WHAT TYPE
OF PERSON ARE YOU?

What are some of your favourite things?

ARE YOU

SLOW-MO

OR DO YOU

GET-UP-AND-GO?

S trategy 11

Activate prior knowledge:
Consider what you already
know about the subject.

ACTIVITY

1 Me, Myself and I

- Read the statements.
- Decide if the statement is true for you.
- List your true statements in columns A, B and C.

1. When your teacher asks a question, you're usually the first to have your hand in the air. **A**

2. For your birthday, you like to go out with your friends and celebrate at the place of your choice. **B**

3. You always make plans for the weekend early in the week. You want to make sure you have something to do. **C**

4. You don't like to make plans too far in advance because you don't know how you'll feel at the time. **A**

5. You have a few different groups of friends that you hang around with depending on what you feel like doing. **B**

6. Your friends depend on you to resolve conflicts and keep peace in the group. **C**

7. For your birthday, you would love to have a surprise party. **A**

8. You don't worry too much about what you'll do on the weekend. Something always turns up. **B**

9. You don't like to take risks. **C**

10. When you watch people face their fears and do crazy things on TV, you wish you were right there with them. **A**

11. Friends describe you as the "life of the party." **B**

12. At lunchtime and during the breaks, you always hang around with the same group of people. **C**

13. There are always people around you. You are never really on your own. **A**

14. You don't mind watching people do crazy things as long as they don't expect you to join them. **B**

15. In class, you don't like to have too much attention on you. You concentrate and try to do your work as well as you can. **C**

16. Your friends expect you to decide what the group's activities will be. **A**

17. You're usually ready to try new things as long as they're within certain limits. **B**

18. The perfect birthday for you is to spend time with one friend and do your favourite activity together. **C**

19. You get bored easily and are always looking for new things to try. **A**

20. When you have a project to do, you don't mind who you work with as long as they take the work seriously. **B**

21. You would never watch a show where people do disgusting things and push themselves to extreme limits. **C**

22. You love to play games like truth or dare. **A**

23. It's easy for you to find things to occupy your time. **B**

24. You are easily influenced by your friends. **C**

- Calculate the number of true answers you have for each letter.
- Find out what your answers show about you. Read the descriptions below.

Mostly As

You're always where the action is. You're very popular and love to be the centre of attention. You're seen as a leader and you like to be in control. You live for the moment and often act on impulse. You'll try just about anything, but you sometimes forget that there are limits to respect.

Mostly Bs

You take an active part in your group. You might not be the leader, but you're the one who makes the party fun! You're very sociable and don't have any problems making friends. You adapt easily to different groups and situations. You're happy to go along with others, but you respect limits.

Mostly Cs

You like safety and security. You like to know what you'll be doing and when. Your presence in your group of friends is very important, but friends won't expect you to take the lead. You don't like to have a lot of attention on you, and you're more comfortable in a one-on-one situation. You're always ready for fun, but you definitely won't go over the edge.

 trategy 18

Scan:
Look or listen for specific information.

 ocabulary 🎧

disgusting *adj.* repugnant
to face your fears *v.* to confront things that you are scared of
to go along with *v.* to agree with
to go over the edge *v.* to go too far

to hang around with *v.* to spend time with
to turn up *v.* to happen
truth or dare *n.* a game where you choose to answer a question correctly or do what someone tells you to do

ACTIVITY 2 Pair and Compare

1 11

- Work with a partner to answer the questions.
- Select your preference for each pair.
- Compare your preferences with your partner's.
- Discover each other's number one preference.

Let's start the quiz. Question number 1. Do you prefer to eat pizza or to eat spaghetti?

That's easy. I prefer to eat pizza.

Me too. I like pizza much better than spaghetti.

---

1. Do you prefer to eat pizza or to eat spaghetti?

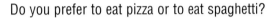

2. Do you prefer to eat popcorn or to eat chips?

3. Do you prefer to have a best friend or to be a best friend?

4. Do you prefer to see your favourite star or to listen to your favourite star?

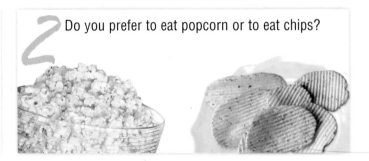

5. Do you prefer to play sports or to watch sports?

6. Do you prefer to bike or to walk?

7. Do you prefer to go on roller coasters or to go on other thrill rides?

8. Do you prefer to skateboard or to snowboard?

Do you prefer to go to the cinema or to rent a movie?

Do you prefer to read books or to read magazines?

Do you prefer to have physical education or to have music class?

Do you prefer to be in math class or to be in English class?

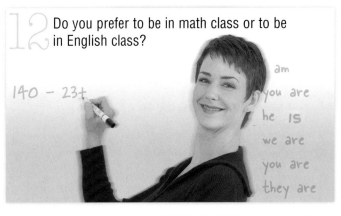

Do you prefer to be at the beach or to be at the pool?

Do you prefer to be in the country or to be in the city?

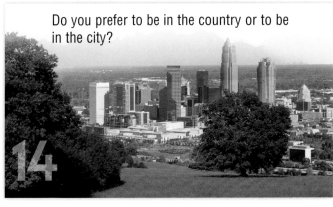

Do you prefer to eat strawberry ice cream or to eat vanilla ice cream?

Do you prefer to eat chocolates or to eat candies?

Strategy 2

Compare:
Note the similarities and differences between two things.

ACTIVITY 3 Get in the Action

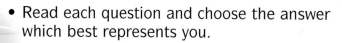

- Read each question and choose the answer which best represents you.

1. How athletic are you?

   a) I play a sport at least three times a week.

   b) I work out twice a week.

   c) I do some sort of exercise once a week.

   d) I watch sports on television every day.

2. Which of the following sounds like more fun for you?

   a) Going to watch a football game with your friends and out for a hamburger afterwards

   b) Playing football with your friends

   c) Going to support your football team by cheering and jumping up and down in the stands

   d) Watching a game on the big screen with lots of great snacks

3. Which of the following represents Canada's food guide to healthy eating for a teenager?

   a) Vegetables and fruit: 2-4 servings

   b) Vegetables and fruit: 4-6 servings

   c) Vegetables and fruit: 5-10 servings

   d) Vegetables and fruit: 5-8 servings

4. You just looked at your schedule for the day and see that you have physical education class. What is your reaction?

   a) Maybe if I pretend to be sick, I'll get to stay home.

   b) I can't wait to get to school. The day is already looking good.

   c) Oh well, it's better than English class.

   d) I don't really mind.

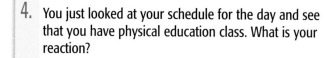

5. School's out for summer. What's your first thought?

   a) Two months of television, movies and computer games

   b) Camping, biking, fresh-air fun with friends

   c) Walking around air-conditioned shopping malls

   d) Great, a different sport for every day!

6. If you were a drink, what would you be?

   a) A sports drink

   b) Soda

   c) Hot chocolate

   d) Water

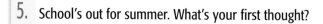

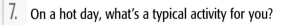

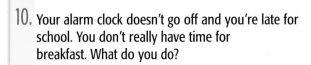

7. On a hot day, what's a typical activity for you?

   a) Staying in an air-conditioned basement, watching television or listening to music

   b) Playing a hard game of soccer to sweat it out

   c) Going for an easy bike ride or a walk with my friends

   d) Hopping in and out of the pool

8. When you go outside in summer, do you wear sunscreen?

   a) Of course. I would never go outside without it.

   b) Yes, when I remember to.

   c) Yes, but only if I'm out between noon and 2 p.m. Those are the most dangerous hours.

   d) No, I don't need to. My skin is really dark. I never burn.

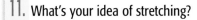

9. What is usually in your lunch box?

   a) I don't usually eat lunch. I eat a big breakfast, and then I snack when I get home from school.

   b) I often buy a sandwich, muffin and yogurt at the cafeteria.

   c) I usually have a sandwich, vegetables and dip, a yogurt, fruit and juice.

   d) I always eat a hot dog and poutine with a soft drink.

10. Your alarm clock doesn't go off and you're late for school. You don't really have time for breakfast. What do you do?

    a) I skip breakfast just this once and eat a big lunch instead.

    b) I take a granola bar and a piece of fruit and eat them on the way to school.

    c) I never eat breakfast.

    d) I drink a big glass of orange juice and eat a big lunch.

11. What's your idea of stretching?

    a) It's what I do in the morning when I get out of bed.

    b) It's when I get up during class to sharpen my pencil after sitting in class for an hour.

    c) It's when I make my allowance last for the whole week.

    d) It's what I do to loosen my muscles before and after exercise.

12. What does winter mean to you?

    a) Warm clothes, warm house, warm fire

    b) Hitting the slopes every weekend for some snowboarding or skiing

    c) An annual trip to the ski slopes

    d) Playing in the snow, making snowmen and skating on the lake

- Count the number of points for each answer.
- To find out what your answers mean, calculate your total using the points below.
- Find out which colour team you are in.
- Team up according to colour. Work with your partners to predict what your results mean.
 • Listen to the descriptions to see if your predictions are correct.

1.	a) 3	b) 2	c) 1	d) 0
2.	a) 1	b) 3	c) 2	d) 0
3.	a) 0	b) 1	c) 3	d) 2
4.	a) 0	b) 3	c) 1	d) 2
5.	a) 0	b) 2	c) 1	d) 3
6.	a) 2	b) 0	c) 1	d) 3
7.	a) 1	b) 0	c) 3	d) 2
8.	a) 3	b) 2	c) 1	d) 0
9.	a) 1	b) 2	c) 3	d) 0
10.	a) 1	b) 3	c) 0	d) 2
11.	a) 1	b) 2	c) 0	d) 3
12.	a) 0	b) 3	c) 1	d) 2

WHAT MY RESULT MEANS

0-12 points	**BLUE**
13-20 points	**RED**
21-28 points	**YELLOW**
29-36 points	**GREEN**

trategy 14

Infer:
Make guesses based on what you already know and on the clues in the text.

ocabulary

allowance *n.* pocket money
I don't mind *idiom* It's not important to me.
to hit the slopes *v.* to go skiing or snowboarding
to loosen *v.* to relax
to pretend *v.* to act as if something is true when it is not
to sharpen *v.* to make pointed
to sweat *v.* to perspire
to work out *v.* to do physical exercises

rammar

ASKING WH- QUESTIONS IN THE SIMPLE PRESENT TENSE
Here are some ways to ask a wh-question in the present tense.

Question word +	present tense verb +	rest of question
Who	plays	soccer?
What	are	the four food groups?
How tall	are	you?
Why	is	it important to stay healthy?

Question word +	auxiliary +	noun/pronoun +	verb +	rest of question
Who	do	you	work out	with?
When	do	you	exercise?	
Where	does	the team	practise	in the winter?
Which	do	you	prefer,	soccer or baseball?
How often	do	you	play	a sport?

FINAL CURTAIN

© 6

Create a class *Quiz Me!* Magazine.

Option **A**

Do you have a partner yet?

Sure. What do you want to do?

Great idea. Let's start.

No, I don't. Do you want to work with me?

Why don't we do a baseball trivia quiz?

1 Find a partner.

2 Choose a subject for your quiz. For example, fashion, food, general information, movies, personality, music, sports, television characters.

3 Choose a format for your quiz. Look at the different quiz types in *Quiz Me!* for ideas.

4 Write ten questions about the subject you chose. Use the information in the grammar box on page 10 for help.

5 Add photos, pictures or illustrations to your quiz.

6 Do your quiz with another pair and find out more about each other.

7 Create a legend to score your quiz. For example,

21-30 points: You're a baseball champion. Super work! Well done.

11-20 points: You're doing very well but you need to learn a bit more about the game.

0-10 points: Too bad. Try again. Maybe you'll do better next time.

Strategies

Remember! Use the strategies you've already practised. Also try

Strategy 8 **Plan:** Think about what you need to do to achieve a goal.
Strategy 22 **Ask for help, repetition, clarification, confirmation:** Request assistance.

Portfolio

Choose items for your portfolio.

FINAL CURTAIN

Design a cover page for *Quiz Me!* magazine.

1 List the subjects of the quizzes in the magazine. For example,

- fashion
- food
- general information
- movies
- personality
- music
- sports
- television characters

2 Write headlines for each quiz. Use the examples in this unit to help you.

3 Design the cover page. Use:

- different fonts or writing styles
- photos, illustrations, pictures

Do you know how to skateboard safely?

ARE YOU A TRUE HORROR MOVIE FAN?

What's your vacation personality?

How much do you know about baseball?

trategies

Remember! Use the strategies you've already practised.
Also try

Strategy 8 **Plan:** Think about what you need to do to achieve a goal.
Strategy 22 Ask for help, repetition, clarification, confirmation: Request assistance.

Portfolio

Choose items for your portfolio.

*It's impossible to move,
to live, to operate at any level
without leaving traces.*

William Gibson

PLACES AND TRACES

Everything disappears over time, so it is important to leave traces for the people of the future. Some people create elaborate time capsules to preserve objects and share what life was like in a particular year or century. But even a family photo album or a package of old letters can help future generations relive the past and understand the lives of their ancestors. Everyone can leave traces of their time and place.

What represents you at this moment?

A. Leave traces of different aspects of your life.

B. Write about yourself for a class capsule.

UNIT 2

trategy 11

Activate prior knowledge:
Consider what you already know about the subject.

Ocabulary

everything *pron.* all things
people *n.* men, women and children
to relive *v.* to experience something that happened in past times
time capsule *n.* a container that is filled with objects from a particular time, to give people in the future an idea of what life was like then

- Find out about a famous time capsule.
- List twenty things that you think are included in the *Crypt of Civilization*.
- Compare your ideas with a partner's ideas.

© 9

Crypt of Civilization
FAMOUS TIME CAPSULE

➤ Thornwell Jacobs inside the chamber.

In 1999, to mark the transition from one millennium to another, many people created time capsules. Individuals, families, schools, communities and even TV casts collected objects to reflect life at this time.

People have preserved memories in different ways for thousands and thousands of years but the term *time capsule* did not exist until 1938. The idea came from Dr. Thornwell Jacobs, the president of an American university. His time capsule is one of the most famous of the twentieth century. It is in Atlanta, Georgia and is called the *Crypt of Civilization*. The container is a swimming pool in an underground room on the university campus. It took Dr. Jacobs three years to collect thousands of objects that represented the previous 6000 years. The crypt was sealed on May 28, 1940.

What will happen if the people of the future don't speak English? Dr. Jacobs thought of that. He included a machine to teach the English language. It contains 1500 key words and uses cartoon instructions that everyone can understand.

Would you like to see what this famous crypt holds? Don't hold your breath. The contents will remain a secret until the crypt is opened on May 28, 8113!

▼ One of the twelve gigantic jars with items from the 1940s. A clock radio and a plastic bowl are visible.

> I think there are books in the crypt.

> I think you're right. And newspapers.

> Me too. And clothes from that time.

Strategy 6

Predict:
Make a hypothesis based on what you already know and on the clues in the text.

Vocabulary

cartoon instructions *n.* instructions in picture form
crypt *n.* an underground room, used in the past for burying people
Don't hold your breath. *idiom* Don't wait anxiously.
underground *adj.* under the earth's surface

ACTIVITY 1 Captivating Capsules

- Look at the contents of two time capsules.
- Choose the more interesting capsule.
- Decide what it shows us about the person who created it or about life in the past.

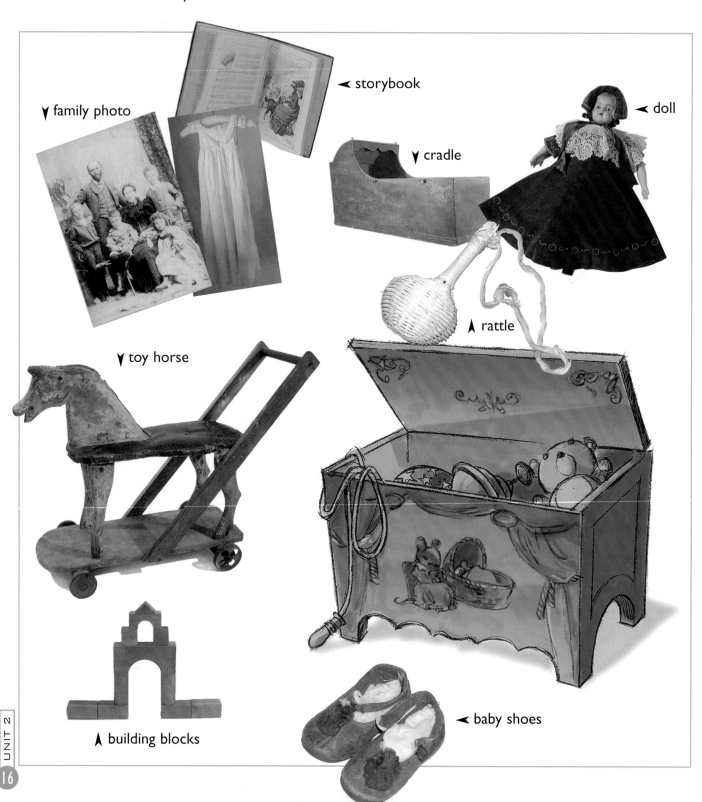

◄ storybook

▼ family photo

◄ doll

▼ cradle

▲ rattle

▼ toy horse

▲ building blocks

◄ baby shoes

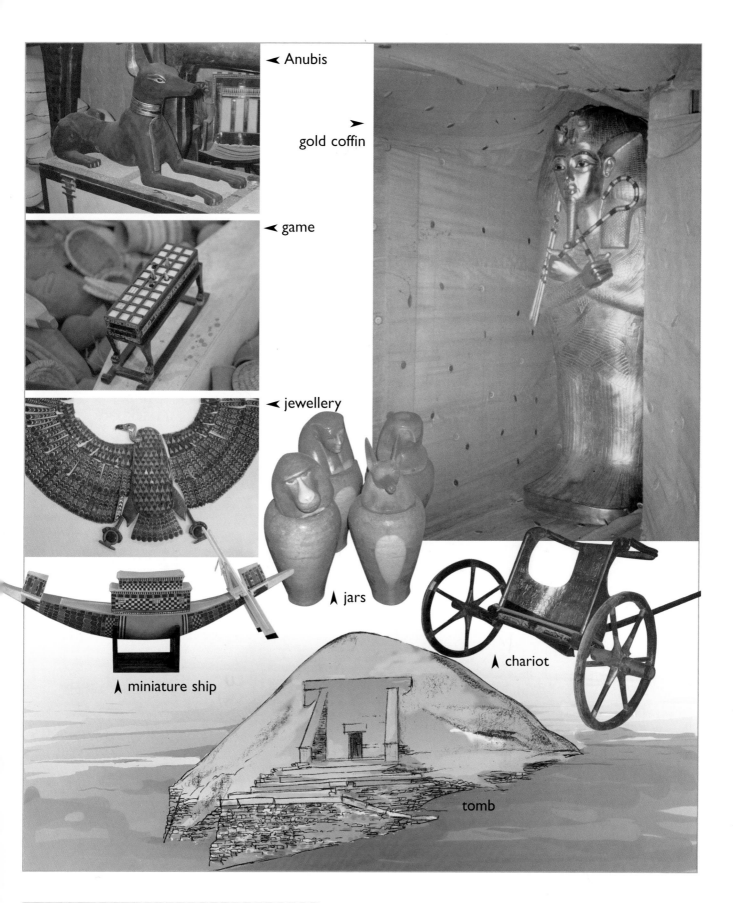

Anubis

gold coffin

game

jewellery

jars

miniature ship

chariot

tomb

ACTIVITY 2 A Picture in Time

- Choose a place or container that holds objects that represent you.
- Draw a picture or take a photo of the container and its contents.
- Label the items.
- Choose five of the items and write down what each one shows about you.

a girl's purse

a boy's sports bag

a backpack

a closet door

a bedroom door

a locker

I took a photo of my locker. You can see my baseball cap. I love wearing a cap but can't wear one in school. I have to leave it in my locker.

Strategy 20

Take notes:
Write down relevant information.

Vocabulary

container *n.* something such as a bag or a box that you keep things in

UNIT 2

18

ACTIVITY 3
Stories of the Past

🎧 • Listen to four people share special memories.

Ⓒ 17

Before you listen
- Read the excerpts.
- Predict what each story is about.

Can you help me? Did Philip say Iceland?

No, Ireland.

O.K. Thanks.

I still remember the smell of those fries and the warm feeling in my tummy when I ate them.

Myriam

This famous ship was built in Belfast, Ireland.

Philip

We loved ending the day this way.

Noëlle

I looked forward to Sundays for that fizzy taste.

Aaron

While you listen
- Listen to the stories.
- Write down the special memory that each person describes.

After you listen
- Check if your predictions were correct.
- Choose the story you liked most and tell a partner why you liked it.
- Tell your partner about a special memory you have of when you were younger.

---

trategy 7

Pay selective attention: Decide what you should pay attention to before you start your work.

ocabulary

excerpt *n.* a short text taken from a longer one
younger *adj.* not as old as you are now
🎧 **beach** *n.* an area of sand next to the sea
country *n.* land that is not near towns or cities
fizzy *adj.* releasing little bubbles

scared *adj.* frightened
ship *n.* a large boat
tummy *n.* child's word for stomach

ACTIVITY

4 Leaving Traces

C 18 21

• Choose a person who will be remembered because of the traces they leave.

My grandmother?
My kindergarten teacher?
My football coach?

Strategy 8

Plan:
Think about what you need to do to achieve a goal.

Vocabulary

to be remembered *v.* to be famous for something important that you did in the past
to be born *v.* to start to exist
happiest *adj.* that gives you the most pleasure
saddest *adj.* that makes you most unhappy

- Try to find interesting information about the person. Look at the questions below for ideas.

- Decide how you will find the information:
  - in an interview with her or him
  - in a book
  - in a magazine
  - on the Internet
  - other

- Write a bio-file for the person.

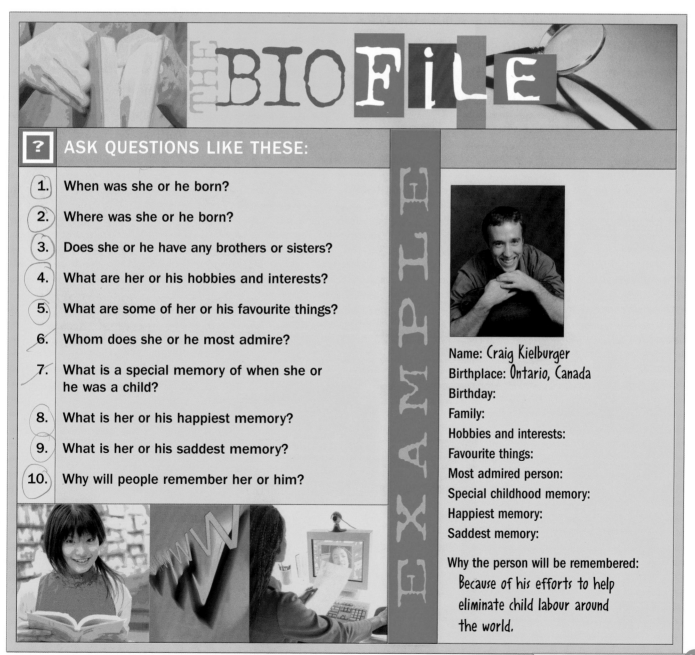

THE BIOFILE

? ASK QUESTIONS LIKE THESE:

1. When was she or he born?

2. Where was she or he born?

3. Does she or he have any brothers or sisters?

4. What are her or his hobbies and interests?

5. What are some of her or his favourite things?

6. Whom does she or he most admire?

7. What is a special memory of when she or he was a child?

8. What is her or his happiest memory?

9. What is her or his saddest memory?

10. Why will people remember her or him?

EXAMPLE

Name: Craig Kielburger
Birthplace: Ontario, Canada
Birthday:
Family:
Hobbies and interests:
Favourite things:
Most admired person:
Special childhood memory:
Happiest memory:
Saddest memory:

Why the person will be remembered:
Because of his efforts to help eliminate child labour around the world.

ACTIVITY

5 Voices of the Present

- Write one question to ask your teacher and one question to ask your partners. (Remember to use the grammar box in Unit 1 to help you ask wh-questions in the present tense.)

- Ask the questions.

- Listen to your partners' questions. Note down each person's answers while you listen.

1. What do you like about school today?

2. What do you dislike about school today?

3. What is your favourite subject?

4. What is a typical school day like for you?

5. How many hours a day do you study or do homework?

1. How are students today different from students five (10, 15, 20) years ago?

2. What was your favourite subject?

3. What did you like best about school?

4. What was the worst thing about school?

5. What time did school start and end?

rammar

ASKING WH- QUESTIONS IN THE SIMPLE PAST TENSE

Here are some ways to ask a wh-question in the past tense.

Question word +	past-tense verb +	rest of question
How	was	your school different from school today?
Who	taught	at your school?

Question word +	auxiliary +	noun/pronoun +	verb +	rest of question
Where	did	you	go	to school?

Strategy 23

Cooperate:
Work with others to achieve a goal.

UNIT 2

FINAL CURTAIN

Leave traces of different aspects of your life.

1 Prepare the following items.
- Your picture of the place that represents you and the description of its contents.
- Your bio-file of a special person.

2 Use your notes from Activity 5 and write a short text about what you want to remember about your school. (Make sure you check and correct your work!)

3 Decide if you will present your items as:
- a poster
- a time capsule
- a CD-ROM
- a multi-media presentation
- other

4 Prepare your presentation.

5 Present the items to your partners.

I like history because . . .

6 Reflect on what you learned about yourself during this activity.
- Think about your personal life, your relationship with your family and friends and your experience at school.
- Write down how you feel.
- Keep this paper to remember how you felt at this moment. (You don't have to show your paper to anyone.)

I like school because
I have friends.
I don't like geography.

---

 trategies

Remember! Use the strategies you've already practised.
Also try

Strategy 10 **Self-monitor:** Check and correct your work.
Strategy 24 **Encourage yourself and others:** Reward yourself and congratulate your classmates.

Portfolio

Choose items for your portfolio.

FINAL CURTAIN

Write about yourself for a class capsule.

Option **B**

1 Create a class capsule.

2 Write a short text about yourself to put in the class capsule. Include:
- your name, age, birthday, physical description, qualities and faults
- the names of your parents, brothers and sisters and best friends
- your favourite hobbies, interests, sports, music, TV shows, movies, clothes, books, food and places
- what you want to achieve this year in your personal life and at school

3 Put your text in an envelope and seal it.

4 Give the envelope to your teacher. Your teacher will return it to you at the end of the school year.

 trategies

Remember! Use the strategies you've already practised. Also try

Strategy 10 **Self-monitor:** Check and correct your work.
Strategy 24 **Encourage yourself and others:** Reward yourself and congratulate your classmates.

Portfolio

Choose items for your portfolio.

*There's a place for us,
Somewhere a place for us.*
Stephen Sondheim

A PLACE FOR US

Teenagers like to be with other teenagers. After school, on the weekend and during holidays, teens need a place to be together. Some teens go to a local shopping mall, some go to their friends' houses and others just meet on a street corner. Some communities try to design places for teenagers. They try to find the right kind of space and the right kind of activities to attract teens. These communities have to ask the question, What makes the ideal teen centre?

What would the best teen centre be like?

A. Design a teen centre.

B. Create a poster for a teen centre.

UNIT 3

Strategy 11

Activate prior knowledge: Consider what you already know about the subject.

Vocabulary

during *prep.* from the beginning to the end of a period of time
kind *n.* type
street corner *n.* a place where roads meet
teenager *n.* someone from the age of 13 to 19, inclusive
together *adv.* with each other

SETTING
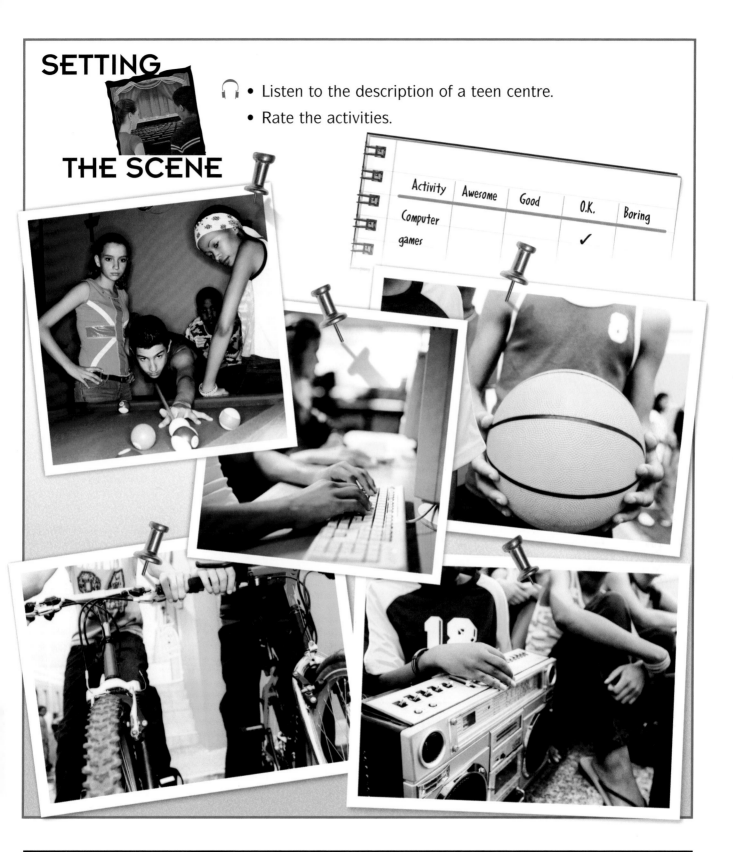

THE SCENE

🎧 • Listen to the description of a teen centre.
• Rate the activities.

Activity	Awesome	Good	O.K.	Boring
Computer games			✔	

trategy 6

Direct attention:
Focus your attention.
Don't be distracted.

ocabulary 🎧

awesome *adj.* very good
boring *adj.* not interesting in any way
computer *n.* an electronic machine that stores information and uses programs to help you find, organize, or change the information

skating rink *n.* a place or building where you can skate
table tennis *n.* an indoor game played on a table by two or four players who hit a small plastic ball to each other across a net

ACTIVITY 1 What Do Teens Want?

- Find out what teens want to do.
- Survey your classmates.

Strategy 12

Compare:
Note the similarities and differences between two things.

Grammar

TALKING ABOUT IMAGINARY FUTURE EVENTS

The pattern for the question form is:

If + [subject] + **could** + [base verb + object], + [question word] + **would** + [subject + base verb]?

If you **could** eat anything for lunch, what **would** you eat?
If Susie **could** watch action movies or cartoons, which **would** she watch?

The pattern for the answer form is:

If + [subject] + **could** + [base verb + object], [subject] + **would/'d** + [subject + base verb]

If I **could** eat anything for lunch, I **would** eat salad.
I would eat salad.
Salad.

If Susie **could** watch action movies or cartoons, she'd watch action movies.
She'd watch action movies.
Action movies.

ACTIVITY 2 Everything in One Place

- Read the article.
- Label the plan of the Teen Zone.

THE LEMMINGWAY GAZETTE

11 MARCH

NEW TEEN CENTRE OPENS IN LEMMINGWAY

Rona Lesley

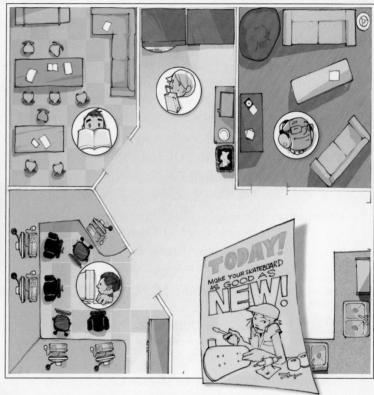

Andrew Winterton, Mayor of Lemmingway, officially opened the town's new youth centre on Saturday. Welcoming guests and local residents to the Teen Zone, Mr. Winterton said, "Our young people need a place where they can get together and have fun. Our parents need to know that their teens are safe. Our whole community has worked hard to build this centre."

The new Teen Zone has everything for teens, from quiet areas to meet friends to a special events room for concerts and courses. Members can watch the latest movies or a favourite program on giant TV screens. There are table-tennis and billiard tables in the games room. For those interested in music, there are CDs with CD players and headphones. Members can also borrow instruments so that they can play their own music. Books and magazines are available in the quiet areas and the computer room offers kids a place to do homework and play games. The refreshment area has soft drinks, a popcorn machine and facilities to prepare meals. Yes, everything a teen needs to hang out with friends is at the Teen Zone.

"This place rocks!" said Matt Wattier and Jodi Vaillancourt. The two teens are working with local business people to build a skatepark at the centre. "And we may raise enough money for a swimming pool," they said, excitedly.

Regional councillor Kim Fortin congratulated the Lemmingway community on their hard work and enthusiasm. "It's wonderful that everyone worked together to create a place for local youth," she said. "Today's teens are tomorrow's parents. If there's nothing to keep them in our small country towns, our communities will die."

Strategy 14

Infer:
Make guesses based on what you already know and on the clues in the text.

Vocabulary

to borrow v. to use something that belongs to someone else and that you must give back to them later
to congratulate v. to tell someone that you are happy because they have achieved something
meal n. breakfast, lunch or dinner
youth n. teenager

ACTIVITY 3

This Week at the Teen Zone

- Read the schedule of events.
- Decide which events you would like to do.

Our Choice
- Pizza Party
- Billiards Challenge

This Week at the TEEN ZONE

Sunday: **Movie Magic.** See the latest hits. Free popcorn.
Pizza Party with music and dancing.

Monday: **Brain Drain:** Play the Brain Drain game with questions only teens can answer. Challenge your knowledge of everything—music, television, sports.
Mandrake's Magic Show. Learn to do magic and enjoy the show.

Tuesday: **Motor Mouth and the Raprats.** Live music.
Basketball Event. Teams, two-on-two events and prizes.

Wednesday: **Starlight Ride.** Take a trip up a mountain on a four-wheeler.
Make-over Class. Sandra and Sam tell teens how to create a cool image.

Thursday: **Video Games Night.** Prizes for highest scores and best team results.
Billiards Challenge. Try our billiards challenge. Prizes for most games played and highest scores.

Friday: **Excursion to Water City.** Sign up for a trip to the biggest water pool, water slide and wave pool in the west.
Friday Night Live. Bring your instrument or borrow a drum and enjoy the fun. You are the star of our group. Soft drinks are free if you play with Maxim's Music Makers. Sing, play or listen.

Saturday: **Midnight Madness.** Come to our Midnight Madness gathering. We have games, pizza, chips, soft drinks and entertainment.
The Games Begin. Try out all our games—table tennis, billiards, minigolf and more.

ACTIVITY 4 — What's for Lunch?

- Read the article.
- Plan a week's menus.

🎧 11

DAY	LUNCH	SNACK
Sunday	Ham or cheese sandwich	Peanut butter cookies
	Coleslaw	Milk or juice
	Fresh fruit	
	Milk or juice	

THE LEMMINGWAY GAZETTE · 12 AUGUST

LUNCHTIME POPULAR AT THE TEEN ZONE CAFÉ

Rona Lesley

Lemmingway's youth centre, the Teen Zone, now has its own café. But it's a café with a difference. Everything is made by Zone members themselves, from locally produced fruit and vegetables.

Each week during the summer, local chef Judith Rowe helps teens create a variety of menus. She helps them understand the value of healthy food and shows them how to create balanced meals. At first Zone members were reluctant to try the meals and snacks. "We wanted fast food," said 14-year-old David White. "But this stuff is really great."

On 19 August local residents will have the opportunity to visit the Zone Café and find out for themselves what the teens have learned. Lunch will be served from 11:30 to 14:30 to raise funds for a skatepark.

What would you like for lunch?

Let's make a pizza.

I'd like a sandwich.

Strategy 18

Scan:
Look or listen for specific information.

Vocabulary

healthy *adj.* good for your body
local *adj.* relating to the particular area you live in
opportunity *n.* a chance to do something
produce *n.* food grown on a farm to be sold
reluctant *adj.* slow and unwilling

ACTIVITY 5 Teens Rule!

- Listen to the students.
- Decide the rules for the Teen Zone.

Vocabulary

fight *n.* a situation in which two people
or groups hurt each other.
garbage *n.* waste material, such as
paper, empty containers and food
thrown away

grammar

WRITING RULES

Rules tell people what to do or what not to do.
They are short and direct. To tell someone what
to do, the pattern is:

Imperative (base) form of the verb + object.
Put things back.

To tell someone what NOT to do, the pattern is:

Do + not (or Don't) + base form of the verb.
Don't throw garbage on the ground.
Or
No + -ing form of the verb.
No fight**ing**.

FINAL CURTAIN

Design a teen centre.

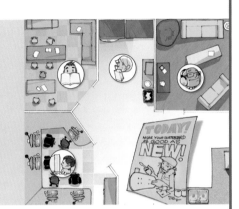

1 Decide on the following for your teen centre:
- activities
- equipment
- food
- rules

2 Decide how you will present the centre. For example, by means of:
- a brochure
- a labelled floor plan
- a multi-media presentation

3 Divide the tasks among the members of your team.

4 Prepare your presentation.

5 Present your teen centre to your classmates.

Welcome to Teen World

6 Consider what you learned during this activity.
- Make a note of new vocabulary.
- Reflect on what you learned about your likes and dislikes and those of your classmates.

trategies

Remember! Use the strategies you've already practised.
Also try

Strategy 8   **Plan:** Think about what you need to do to achieve a goal.
Strategy 23   **Cooperate:** Work with others to achieve a goal.

Portfolio

Choose items for your portfolio.

FINAL CURTAIN

Create a poster for a teen centre.

1 Choose an area in a teen centre. For example:
- computer room
- games room
- quiet room

2 Make a list of the equipment you will need in your area.

3 Prepare a poster about the area.

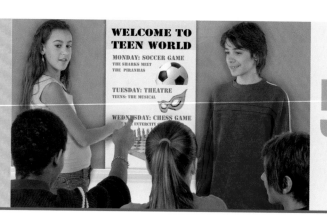

4 Present your poster to your classmates.

5 Consider what you learned during this activity.
- Make a note of new vocabulary.
- Reflect on what you learned about your likes and dislikes and those of your classmates.

---

 trategies

Remember! Use the strategies you've already practised.
Also try

Strategy 8   Plan: Think about what you need to do to achieve a goal.

Portfolio

Choose items for your portfolio.

*Share our similarities,
celebrate our differences.*
M. Scott Peck

LET'S CELEBRATE

Every season has its celebrations and every celebration has a reason. Some celebrations are small and personal, like birthdays and anniversaries. Others are large and shared by a group, like Thanksgiving and Valentine's Day. Canadians come from many parts of the world and bring their celebrations with them. Small or large, every celebration adds to our culture and heritage.

What do you celebrate?

A. Create a We Celebrate display.

B. Design a greeting card for a special celebration.

 trategy 11

Activate prior knowledge: Consider what you already know about the subject.

 ocabulary

anniversary *n.* a date that is special because it is exactly a year or a number of years after an important event

birthday *n.* the date in each year on which you were born

SETTING THE SCENE

- Find out what events your classmates celebrate.
- Place the celebrations on your calendar.

Which events do we celebrate in summer?

Right. That's July 1. And I celebrate my birthday. Can we put that?

August 8. When's your birthday?

What about Canada Day?

Sure. It's a celebration. When is it?

December 31, in the middle of winter.

Strategy 23

Cooperate:
Work with others to achieve a goal.

Vocabulary

summer *n.* the season between spring and autumn (June, July, August in Canada)
winter *n.* the season between autumn and spring (December, January, February in Canada)

LET'S CELEBRATE **37**

ACTIVITY

1 Autumn Is Awesome

 • Listen to the announcement.
- Add the events to your calendar.
- Make notes for a poster.
- Compare the events.

Dates and times will be posted soon.

coming Events

AUTUMN IS AWESOME AT PAUL YUZYK HIGH SCHOOL.

Come celebrate with local students this fall.

EVENT	HOSTED BY	MORE INFORMATION
Rosh Hashanah		Party

---

§trategy 12

Compare:
Note the similarities and differences between two or more things.

℧ocabulary

candle *n.* a long piece of wax with a piece of string through the middle, which you burn to use as a light

date *n.* a small sweet brown fruit

ℊrammar

TALKING ABOUT FUTURE EVENTS

We use **will** + the base form of the verb to express future time.
    I **will go** to the Ramadan evening.

The short form of **will** is **'ll** .
    She **will** celebrate her birthday soon
    She**'ll** celebrate her birthday soon.

The short form of **will not** is **won't**.
    Kate **will not** be at the Halloween dance.
    Kate **won't** be at the Halloween dance.

ACTIVITY 2 Winter Is Wild

- Read about some more celebrations.
- Add them to your calendar.
- Make a scrapbook page about a winter celebration.

Kwanzaa

We spent our winter vacation with some African-Canadian friends to celebrate Kwanzaa. Kwanzaa is an African-American holiday which celebrates family, community and culture. The name comes from the first harvest celebrations of Africa. The phrase *matunda ya kwanza* means "first fruits" in Swahili, the most widely spoken African language.

We lit candles of black, red and green: black for the African people, red for their struggle and green for the future and for hope. We ate African food and then we danced.

We celebrated from December 26 to January 1. It was great fun.

ROBBIE BURNS NIGHT

Burns Night celebrates the birth of Scotland's national poet. At the traditional supper, the men wear kilts. A piper plays bagpipes as a special meat pudding called a haggis is carried in. Robbie Burns' poems are read out loud.

QUEBEC WINTER CARNIVAL

This is a cool celebration of winter! The settlers of New France continued the tradition of getting together just before Lent to eat, drink and be merry. The first Quebec Winter Carnival was held in 1894. Now it's the largest winter carnival in the world.

The carnival lasts for about fifteen days but we were only there from January 28 to 30. We went skating and ice fishing. We visited an ice tower and took a ride in a sleigh pulled by a horse. Fortunately, we were covered with warm blankets! We watched a huge parade at night and then went to see the wonderful ice sculptures. My sister loved the lights on the ice but she refused to try the ice slide with me.

---

 trategy 17

Recombine:
Try to combine, in a new way, the words and expressions you already know.

 ocabulary

bagpipe *n.* a traditional Scottish instrument
harvest *n.* when grain, vegetables, etc. are collected from the fields
sleigh *n.* a vehicle for travelling on snow
struggle *n.* a fight

ACTIVITY 3 Spring Swings

- Read the text.
- Write a short verse for a spring celebration.

Spring is a season of new beginnings. People around the world celebrate spring in many different ways. The Irish celebrate St. Patrick's Day. In Britain, spring is welcomed with dancing and village festivals on May 1. Christians celebrate Easter and Jews observe Passover. Chinese families get together for the Spring Festival, the most important Chinese festival. Mother's Day is also celebrated in May.

SWING INTO SPRING!
SEND A GREETING.

HAPPY ST. PATRICK'S DAY

HAPPY MOTHER'S DAY

HAPPY PASSOVER

Mom
Thanks for cooking my meals
Thanks for washing my clothes
Thanks for giving me kisses
Thanks for all of those.

Grass grows
Birds sing
Snow melts
It's spring

---

 trategy 3

Rephrase:
Use different words to say the same thing.

 ocabulary

beginning *n.* a start
to welcome *v.* to greet

FINAL CURTAIN

Create a *We Celebrate* display.

1 Think of all the events you and your classmates celebrate.

2 Place the events on a calendar and illustrate it.

3 Label a map showing where each celebration originated.

Kwanzaa

May Day

4 Briefly describe each event.

5 Consider what you learned during this activity.

6 Make a note of new vocabulary.

---

 trategies

Remember! Use the strategies you've already practised.
Also try

Strategy 10 **Self-monitor:** Check and correct your work.
Strategy 21 **Use semantic mapping:** Group similar ideas together.

Portfolio

Choose items for your portfolio.

FINAL CURTAIN

Design a greeting card for a special celebration.

1 Choose your favourite celebration.

2 Create a greeting card for the celebration.

3 Decorate your card with photos or drawings.

4 Write a message inside.

5 Share your card with your classmates.

6 Consider what you learned during this activity.

---

trategies

Remember! Use the strategies you've already practised.
Also try

Strategy 10   **Self-monitor:** Check and correct your work.
Strategy 21   **Use semantic mapping:** Group similar ideas together.

Portfolio

Choose items for your portfolio.

*There's nothing wrong
with teenagers that
twenty years won't cure*
Anon.

DO YOU SPEAK ADULT?

Adults and teenagers sometimes seem to speak different languages. Teenagers often say that their parents and teachers don't understand them. Parents often complain that young people never listen. Adults may criticize the way teens dress, talk and act. They sometimes say that the music teens like is just noise and not music. Teens may think that the music adults listen to is boring. Sometimes it seems that teens and adults share little more than the air they breathe. Can adults and teens learn to understand each other better? Can they learn to speak each other's language?

How can adults and teenagers understand each other?

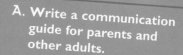

A. Write a communication guide for parents and other adults.

B. Write a postcard to your parent or another adult.

Strategy 19	**V**ocabulary
Skim: Read through a text quickly to get a general overview.	**to criticize** *v.* to say that someone or something is bad in some way **to listen** *v.* to try to hear and understand sounds or what someone is saying **noise** *n.* a loud or annoying sound **to seem** *v.* to appear **to understand** *v.* to comprehend

SETTING THE SCENE

- Create a dictionary of emotions.
  - Write the emotion words in your notebook.
  - Define or illustrate each one.
  - Add other emotion words during the year.

- Choose five words that describe the way you feel when you talk to adults.

trategy 26

Take risks:
Experiment and don't be afraid to make mistakes.

When I talk to adults I often feel angry. But sometimes I'm cheerful.

Emotion Dictionary

Word	Meaning
Angry	mad
Annoyed	impatient
Bored	not interested
Cheerful	happy

ACTIVITY 1 Say What You Mean

- Do you know what adults **really** mean?
- Take a quiz and find out.

QUIZ 1 What Do Adults Really Mean?

When adults (usually your parents) say

Where are you going?

they mean

a) Is it safe?

b) I'm sure it's bad.

Who are you going with?

they mean

a) Do I know them?

b) Are they wild?

You're grounded.

they mean

a) You broke the rules, now you have to take the consequences.

b) I can't control you.

When adults (usually your parents) say

Is that what you're wearing?

they mean

a) I don't like that style.

b) You'll embarrass me.

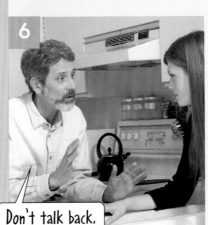

That music is too loud.

they mean

a) I need some quiet time.

b) Your music is terrible.

Don't talk back.

they mean

a) I deserve your respect.

b) What I say is the law and there's no use saying anything.

When adults (usually your parents) say

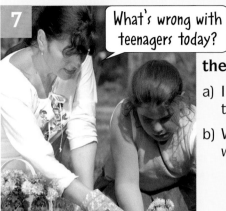

7

What's wrong with teenagers today?

they mean

a) I wasn't like that.

b) What's wrong with you?

8

Have a good time.

they mean

a) Stay safe.

b) Don't embarrass me.

9

Be home by midnight.

they mean

a) You need your sleep.

b) Teens always get into trouble after midnight.

- Now design a quiz to find out if adults understand what teenagers mean.

Quiz 2: What Do Teens Really Mean?

When teenagers say	they mean
1. You treat me like a child.	a) You don't trust me.
	b) I want to do what I wa[nt]
2. I can't talk to you.	a)
	b) I don't want to talk to y[ou]
3. Leave me alone	a)
	b) I have something to hide.
4. This homework is stupid.	a)
	b) I don't want to do it.

trategy 20

Stall for time:
Show that you need more time to think of your response.

ocabulary

to ground *v.* to make someone stay at home as a punishment
safe *adj.* not likely to cause any physical injury or harm
to talk back *v.* to answer rudely
wild *adj.* out of control

ACTIVITY 2 Teen Talk

🎧 • Listen to the talk show.

ⓒ 3 13
• Make notes about each call.
• Create your own call-in show.

Caller #1: Helen
Problem:
Parents embarrass her,
ask friends questions.
Advice:

Hello. Welcome to Teens Talk.

Do your parents drive you crazy?
Do other adults bug you?

Can teens and adults ever communicate?

Call us with your stories. Our lines are open.

Hello. Who's calling, please?

Hi. My name's Helen.
May I speak to Jocelyne, please?

Sure. Hold on a minute.

UNIT 5

48

ACTIVITY

3 Ask Nicely

- Read the messages from concerned adults.
- Decide what advice to give them.

ASK DR. T.

ASK DR. T.

WORRIED

From: Worried
To: Dr. T.

Dear Dr. T.,

My daughter wants to go to a party with a much older boy. I want to meet him and know that she will be safe. How should I ask her about him?

Worried Mom

OVERWORKED PARENTS

From: Overworked Parents
To: Dr. T.

Dear Dr. T.,

We have a busy life and there are many jobs to do around the house. Our children don't do even the simplest things, like putting away their dirty dishes. How can we make them understand that we need their help?

Overworked Parents

TROUBLED TEACHER

From: Troubled Teacher
To: Dr. T.

Dear Dr. T.,

I teach in a small school. I have many wonderful students but I have a problem with some of them. They use very bad language, even during class. What should I do to help them stop?

Troubled Teacher

---

ar Worried,

u should tell your daughter why you want
o know about this boy. Don't ask too many
questions. Just ask a few important ones.

Dr. T.

INTERNET DAD

From: Internet Dad
To: Dr. T.

Dear Dr. T.,

Our son and daughter argue about the Internet every night and all weekend. I want them to use the Internet but I worry about the chat rooms. I have two problems: stopping the arguing and keeping them safe. Do you have any advice?

Internet Dad

LOCKED OUT

From: Locked Out
To: Dr. T.

Dear Dr. T.,

My son is 14 years old and locks himself in his room every night. I'm worried about him. How can I get him to join the family in the evening?

Locked Out

---

 trategy 17

Recombine:
Try to combine, in a new way, the words and expressions you already know.

 ocabulary

to argue v. to disagree with someone in words, often in an angry way
bad language n. swearing
chat room n. a place on the Internet where you can send and receive instant messages
job n. a task
to lock v. to close a door so that no one can enter

 rammar

GIVING ADVICE

We often use the word **should** when we ask for advice or give advice.

Question
Question word + **should** + noun/pronoun + verb (+ rest of sentence)
What **should** I do about this problem?

Answer
Noun/Pronoun + **should** + verb (+ rest of sentence)
You **should** tell your daughter how you feel.
Parents **should** try to communicate with their children.

ACTIVITY 4 I Didn't Mean That

- Practise talking to adults.
- Prepare a role play with your partners.

> Why do I have to baby-sit? I hate staying home on Friday night.

> We can't leave your brother alone.

> Look, we have to visit Grandma.

> All right. But can I go to the dance when you get back?

Situation Card
Getting Permission to go to a school dance

Emotion Card
Frustrated

grammar

CHECKING COMPREHENSION

A good way to check that you've understood what someone says is to repeat what you think you heard. This is called **echoing**.

They say
I want you to stay home tonight.
You say
You want me to stay home tonight?
They say
Please take out the garbage before you call Katie.
You say
The garbage? or Before I call Katie?

strategy 8

Plan:
Think about what you need to do to achieve a goal.

FINAL CURTAIN

Write a communication guide for parents and other adults.

1 Decide which situations to include in the communication guide.

Asking for a lift
Sleeping over at a friend's
Staying up late
Asking for money

2 Choose one of the situations.

I want to write about visiting family.

3 Write a page about the situation.

1. TEEN: I don't want to go to Aunt Barb's for Thanksgiving. It's boring. I'm not going.
2. PARENT: Oh yes you are, young lady.
3. TEEN: You're not my boss. I'm not going and you can't make me.
4. PARENT: Don't speak to me like that. You're going, and that's final.
5. TEEN: I hate you. Thanksgiving sucks.

1. TEEN: I don't want to go to Aunt Barb's for Thanksgiving. It's boring. I'm not going.
2. PARENT: You don't want to go?
3. TEEN: No. There's no one my age.
4. PARENT: But the food is great. And everyone loves seeing you.
5. TEEN: I guess. But can I bring a DVD or video game to play after dinner?

4 Edit your partner's work.

5 Present your page to the class.

Talking to Teens

---

trategies

Remember! Use the strategies you've already practised.
Also try

Strategy 1 **Gesture:** Use actions to help transmit your message.
Strategy 10 **Self-monitor:** Check and correct your work.
Strategy 15 **Practise:** Reuse language until you get it right.

Portfolio

Choose items for your portfolio.

My Portfolio

FINAL CURTAIN

Write a postcard to your parent or another adult.

Option B

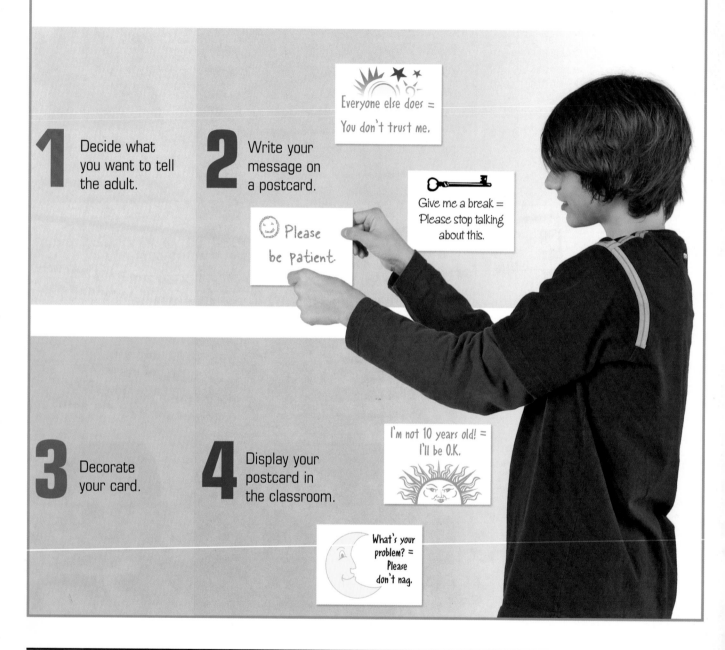

1 Decide what you want to tell the adult.

2 Write your message on a postcard.

Everyone else does = You don't trust me.

Give me a break = Please stop talking about this.

☺ Please be patient.

3 Decorate your card.

4 Display your postcard in the classroom.

I'm not 10 years old! = I'll be O.K.

What's your problem? = Please don't nag.

Strategies

Remember! Use the strategies you've already practised.
Also try

Strategy 10 **Self-monitor:** Check and correct your work.
Strategy 15 **Practise:** Reuse language until you get it right.

Portfolio

Choose items for your portfolio.

*We are living on this planet
as if we had another one
to go to.*
Paul Connett

CONTAMI-NATION

It seems that people have been talking about environmental problems forever. Water pollution, ground pollution, air pollution, the greenhouse effect, the list goes on and on. Just as we start to find possible solutions for some problems, new ones appear. We are creating a contaminated nation.

Will we ever find solutions to these problems, or has saving the environment become a superhuman task?

A. Make a Contami-Nation comic strip.

B. Make a Contami-Nation character card.

UNIT 6

 trategy 14

Infer:
Make guesses based on what you already know and on the clues in the text.

 ocabulary

greenhouse effect *n.* a problem caused by pollution, which stops the sun's heat from escaping and causes the air around the Earth to become warmer

SETTING THE SCENE

- List all the words you know about the environment.
- Look at the photos for help.
- Begin a green glossary.

6

GREEN GLOSSARY

smog: a mixture of smoke, fog and pollution in the atmosphere

I'll write down our ideas. You can be the speaker.

Does this look O.K.?

Excellent. Let's make an idea web. Write "environment" in a circle, and then we can write other words around it.

That's great. Now, what environmental problems do you know of?

Strategy 11

Activate prior knowledge: Consider what you already know about the subject.

Vocabulary

green *adj.* connected with the environment or its protection

ACTIVITY 1

Waste Not, Want Not

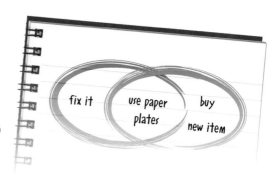

fix it   use paper   buy
          plates   new item

- Think about how your daily actions help or hurt the environment.
- Answer the questions below.
- Work with a partner to make a Venn diagram to show your similarities and differences.

There are certain things we can control and others that we can't. Often, industries are blamed for air pollution, the depletion of the ozone layer, global warming and smog. You should be aware of these problems and be sensitive to them, but let's look at what you can control in your everyday life.

1. When you break something, do you try to fix it or do you buy a new item?

2. What do you do with your old clothes and/or accessories?

3. What do you do with your old computers, music players, cell phones and video games?

4. When you have a party, do you use plastic, paper or ordinary plates?

5. Do you buy new school supplies each year or use left-overs from the year before?

6. Do you usually write on both sides of a sheet of paper?

7. You have just started the good copy of something and you make a mistake. Do you erase it, or do you scrap the paper and start again on a new sheet?

8. In your lunch box, do you usually have disposable packages or reusable containers?

9. Do you use a lot of disposable items (plastic sandwich bags, paper cups, paper plates, wet wipes, soap dispensers etc.)?

10. Do you use excessive amounts of toilet paper?

11. Do you usually have large amounts of clothing in your laundry basket?

12. While you brush your teeth, do you turn off the tap?

13. How long does your average shower last?

14. Do you keep cold water in the fridge or do you run the tap for each glass until the water is cold enough?

15. Do you go to school by bus, car, bicycle, scooter or on foot?

Did you know...?

1. An average Canadian uses 335 L of water per day.

2. About two-thirds of indoor water use at home is in the bathroom.

3. Most toilets use 40% more water than is necessary.

4. When garbage decomposes, it produces two greenhouse gases: carbon dioxide and methane.

5. Sometimes garbage is incinerated to help clear landfills. This creates other pollution risks: ash, carbon dioxide and acidic gases and chemicals.

> The best way to help the environment is to reduce, reuse and recycle.

Strategy 12

Compare:
Note the similarities and differences between two or more things.

Vocabulary

to break *v.* to damage
disposable *adj.* designed to be used for a short time and then thrown away
laundry basket *n.* a container for clothes etc. that need to be washed

leftovers *n.* things that remain
to run the tap *v.* to leave the tap open
to scrap *v.* to throw away
to waste *v.* to use more than necessary
Waste not, want not *idiom* If you don't waste things, you'll have enough.

ACTIVITY 2 Turning Trash to Treasure

- Read the text and look at the illustrations.
- Think of things that are found in the garbage.
- Choose five objects and suggest another use for each one.

ITEMS	USE
wine corks	hot pad
Old chair	
Flower pot	
Doll's pram	
Dresser drawer	

TURNING TRASH TO TREASURE

Garbage doesn't have to be just garbage. Many people use their imagination to transform old objects into wonderful new creations. One artist makes works of art from old metal cooking pots. Another makes jewellery from bottle tops. Shops sell photo frames covered in mosaics. You can make the same thing using broken CDs or leftover bathroom tiles. An old skateboard can become an interesting shelf. Some people make musical instruments from recycled materials. Cardboard boxes and rubber bands can be turned into a guitar. Coffee cans and yogurt pots make great drums. From coasters made out of old CDs to a desk organizer from cardboard tubes, the possibilities are endless. People have even managed to build houses with reused materials. With imagination and creativity, anything is possible.

---

 trategy 25

Lower anxiety:
Relax. Laugh. Remember your successes and focus on your progress.

 ocabulary

cooking pot *n.* a metal container for heating food
jewellery *n.* things that you wear for decoration, such as rings and necklaces
shelf *n.* a board to put things on, fixed to a wall or in a closet
tile *n.* a square piece of a hard material that is used for covering roofs, walls or floors
trash *n.* garbage, rubbish

ACTIVITY

3 School: A Dangerous Dump?

 7

- List what kinds of garbage you expect to find inside and outside your school.

- See which of these things you can find.

- Display your results in school. For example:
  - put them in a table
  - make a poster
  - make a video

OBJECT	DESCRIPTION OF THE OBJECT	WHERE I FOUND IT	WHAT I DID WITH IT
can	soft drink	on the cafeteria floor	put it in the recycling bin

SCHOOL YARD OR SCHOOL DUMP?

Thanks, I didn't see it.

Watch out! That's broken glass.

And be careful when you pick it up. It's dangerous.

Watch out! The school is becoming a dump.
Be careful! Garbage can be dangerous.
Please use the garbage and recycling bins.
Everybody needs to do their part.

trategy 23

Cooperate:
Work with others to achieve a goal.

ocabulary

bin *n.* a large container
scavenger hunt *n.* a game in which people try to find different objects
waste *n.* material which has been made useless

CONTAMI-NATION **61**

ACTIVITY 4 Techno-Waste

- Read about a new pollution problem.
- List all the electronic equipment that you own personally or have in your home.
- Beside each item, identify whether it is a want or a need and explain why.

ITEM	WANT	NEED	WHY?
computer		✔	

TECHNOLOGICAL PROGRESS OR ENVIRONMENTAL POISON?

In the 21st century, technology is progressing at an incredible speed. The number of electronic devices available to us is increasing faster than we could ever have imagined. New items are appearing on the market every day. Cell phones, desktops, laptops, hand-held computers, printers, keyboards, monitors, cameras and more are improving almost instantly. These inventions are making our lives a lot easier, but will there be a price to pay for all this convenience?

People are buying more and more to keep up with all the latest models and developments. Advertisers are encouraging us to buy more recent versions of equipment that is often still in excellent condition. With our excessive consumption, we are causing and contributing to new environmental problems. Electronic waste is particularly dangerous because of the chemicals and metals, such as lead and mercury, that the equipment contains. We are creating a contaminated nation.

How can we help find a solution to this problem? The first thing we can do is reuse the equipment we no longer need by donating it to charity or selling it in a garage sale. This extends the equipment's use, but it still doesn't solve the problem of where it will go when it is no longer useful. Some recycling plants take electronic equipment apart and make sure that it is disposed of in ways that will have a minimal risk for the environment. For now, though, electronic waste is growing rapidly and the solutions to the problem are still to be found.

Can we make a difference? Absolutely. The question we should ask is, "Do I really need that new cell phone or computer?" We need to think twice before replacing our "old" equipment and only buy what we really need.

trategy 18

Scan:
Look or listen for specific information.

ocabulary

available *adj.* able or ready to be used
keyboard *n.* all the keys on a computer that you press to make it work
to take apart *v.* to break into its components

rammar

TALKING ABOUT TEMPORARY ACTIONS

The present progressive is used for actions that are temporary or are taking place at the moment of speaking.

For example,
> The students **are reading** a text about techno-waste.

It is also used to describe a trend.

For example,
> More and more teenagers **are using** cell phones.

To form the present progressive, use
the auxiliary **to be** and the **main verb** + **ing**.

I	am				
You	are				
He/she/it	is	+	read	+	ing.
We	are				
You	are				
They	are				

ACTIVITY

5 The Pollution Problem

9

- Listen to the interviews.
- Decide which forms of pollution are described and give the example of each one.
- Say what you think about the different types of pollution.

> Do you think using bad language is a form of pollution?

> I'm not sure. It's hard to say. I agree that it's just words but we should respect other people's opinions.

> No, I totally disagree. Words are just words. What's your opinion?

FINAL CURTAIN

Create a *Contami-Nation* comic strip.

Option A

Aquaman

Toxic Waste

Waste-eater

Dr. Paul Ooshan

1 Choose one of these characters or create your own.

2 Decide on the character's mission and special abilities.

Mission: to reduce garbage in schoolyard

Special abilities: dynamic leader, determined, can influence people

3 Write a story starring your character.
- Where does the story take place?
- What happens?
- Who are the other characters?
- Does the story demonstrate your character's mission and abilities?

4 Divide the story into scenes of the main events.
- Who is in each scene?
- What are the characters saying?
- What are the characters doing?
- What is the scenery?

5 Compose your comic strip.
- Draw one square for each scene.
- Draw the characters and scenery.
- Write the speech in bubbles. Remember to use the words in your green glossary for help.

6 Present your finished comic strip to the class.

trategies

Remember! Use the strategies you've already practised.
Also try

Strategy 20 Take notes: Write down relevant information.
Strategy 21 Use semantic mapping: Group similar ideas together.

Portfolio

Choose items for your portfolio.

FINAL CURTAIN

Make a *Contami-Nation* character card.

Aquaman

Dr. Paul Ooshan

Waste-eater

Toxic Waste

1
- Choose one of these characters, or create your own.
- Choose the character's **name**.

2 Decide on the character's **mission or goal**. What does the character want to achieve?

3 Decide on the character's **strengths or qualities**. What is he or she able to do?

4 What **obstacles** does the character have to overcome? What problems will he or she have to face?

5 Write a **strategy or plan**. How will the character solve the environmental problem?

6 Provide an illustration of your character.

7 Present your character to your classmates. Remember to use the words in your green glossary for help.

Mission:
to reduce garbage in schoolyard
Special abilities:
dynamic leader, determined, can influence people
Obstacles:
1) Students throw garbage on ground at lunchtime.
2) Students use disposable containers.
Strategy/plan:
a) Set up pollution patrol in schoolyard at lunchtime.
b) Hold campaign to encourage students to use reusable containers.

Strategies

Remember! Use the strategies you've already practised. Also try

Strategy 20 Take notes: Write down relevant information.
Strategy 21 Use semantic mapping: Group similar ideas together.

Portfolio

Choose items for your portfolio.

My Portfolio

*When the going gets tough,
the tough get going.*
Danish proverb

DEALING WITH DISASTER

Sometimes terrible things happen in the world. Some of these disasters are caused by the forces of nature; some are caused by human beings. Some are accidents and, unfortunately, some are deliberate. Some disasters are local, others are international. There are some disasters that are so shocking that people always remember where they were and what they we doing when they heard the news. We can learn a great deal about people from their responses to disasters. What disasters do you remember? How did you react?

What should we do in emergencies?

A. Prepare an emergency reponse plan.

B. Describe a disaster you have experienced.

Strategy 11

Activate prior knowledge:
Consider what you already know about the subject.

Vocabulary

deliberate *adj.* planned, not by accident
to remember *v.* to call to mind
shocking *adj.* very upsetting

SETTING THE SCENE

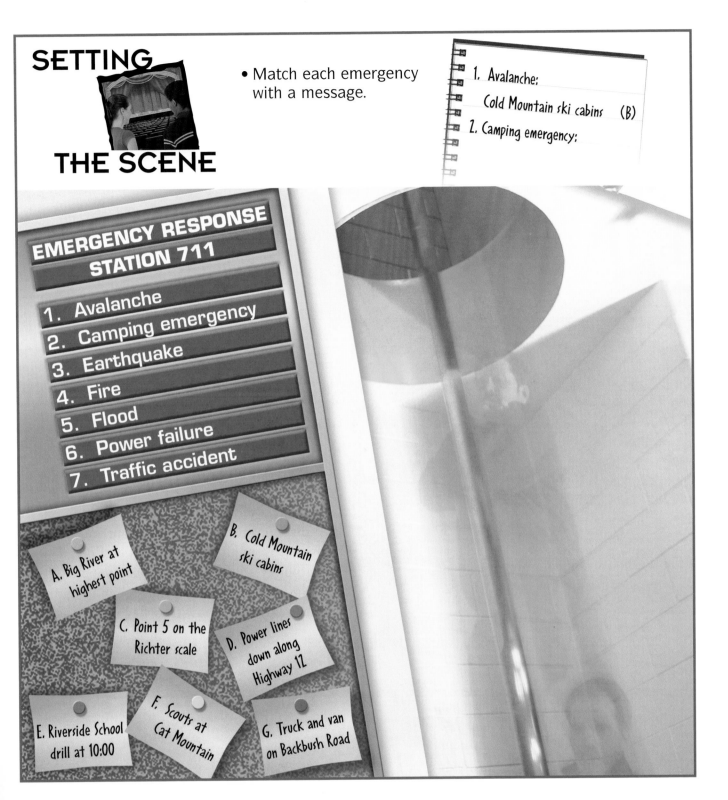

• Match each emergency with a message.

1. Avalanche:
   Cold Mountain ski cabins   (B)
2. Camping emergency:

EMERGENCY RESPONSE STATION 711

1. Avalanche
2. Camping emergency
3. Earthquake
4. Fire
5. Flood
6. Power failure
7. Traffic accident

A. Big River at highest point

B. Cold Mountain ski cabins

C. Point 5 on the Richter scale

D. Power lines down along Highway 12

E. Riverside School drill at 10:00

F. Scouts at Cat Mountain

G. Truck and van on Backbush Road

---

 trategy 14

Infer:
Make guesses based on what you already know and on the clues in the text.

 ocabulary

earthquake *n.* a sudden shaking of the earth's surface
emergency *n.* an unexpected and dangerous situation that must be dealt with immediately
flood *n.* a very large amount of water that covers an area that is usually dry
power failure *n.* a period of time when there is no electricity supply
Richter scale *n.* a system of numbers used for measuring how powerful an earthquake is
traffic *n.* the vehicles moving along a street

ACTIVITY 1 In the News

- Read the accounts of some famous disasters.
- Answer the following questions about each event.
  - What happened?
  - Where did it happen?
  - When did it happen?
- Write notes about a local disaster.

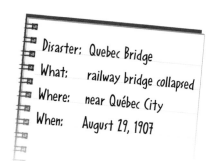

Disaster: Quebec Bridge
What: railway bridge collapsed
Where: near Québec City
When: August 29, 1907

August 20, 1996

Fifteen days ago the people of the Saguenay faced a regional disaster. The flood waters washed away a shopping complex, homes and cars. 12,000 people ran from their homes. There were millions of dollars in damage. Sadly, there were 10 deaths.

The residents of three communities in the Saguenay were affected by the flood. News of the disaster brought an immediate and generous response from all parts of Canada. Food, clothes and money came from ordinary people. It will take a long time for the Saguenay to return to normal, but they know they have help.

August 29, 1907

Today our greatest bridge is our saddest disaster. The bridge was not completely up when it fell down. Authorities have accused Theodore Cooper, the engineer in charge of construction and design, of incompetence. Mr. Cooper states that the facts will show that he is not to blame.

On June 15 inspectors noticed that two of the large steel support beams were misaligned.

Two days ago, these beams seemed bent. Mr. Cooper did not stop work on the bridge.

Today, the beams shook. With a terrible noise the bridge plunged into the waters below. Seventy-five construction workers lost their lives.

OL. CXXXVI., NO. 20

UEBEC BRIDGE

COLLAPSES

---

ty-Four Men Perish in
the Disaster.

NY OTHERS HURT

---

nded Men Pinned in
the Wreckage Near
the Shore.

CUERS CAN'T REACH THEM.

---

s and Shrieks Heard by the
wds at Riverside, Who Have
Leave Victims to Their Fate.
nds of Lamentation From
dows and Orphans in Little
lage Homes—But Eight of the
ety-Two Workers Were Re-
ed Alive—Crash Heard in
ebec City and People Thought
ere Was an Earthquake—Pro-
ty Loss $2,000,000.

(Special to The Gazette.)
bec, August 29.—The great Que-
bridge collapsed this afternoon,
ow the vast mass of steel work
tangled wreck across the St.
ence channel, while so far as can
imated eighty-four men have lost
lives. The bridge fell at exactly
y-three minutes to six this even-
ust as many of the workmen
preparing to leave. The disaster
however, so horribly effective in
g out the lives of the men em-
d on it that very little is known
how it happened, as those who
ft are completely benumbed by
rror of the catastrophe and can
kle to aid the situation.

as the southern extension of the
which collapsed, and this was
y nearing the zenith of the im-
steel arch which was to span the
For eight hundred feet from
ore the massive structure reared
, with no supports but the piers
the shore, and one pier erected
river, while the outward ex-
denly those on the northern shore
he end of the half arch bend down
, and a moment later the whole
ous fabric began to break down.

June 1, 1914

The *Empress of Ireland* sank on May 29. The 465 survivors are in Rimouski. There were over 1400 passengers and crew on the ship, including 170 members of the Salvation Army. Authorities reported that another ship hit the *Empress* around midnight. Two small ships raced to the scene and saved about 400 people. Local people waited for these survivors at the pier in Rimouski. They had warm clothes and hot drinks for the survivors. The captains of both ships were obviously inexperienced. This is a disaster that could have been prevented.

SALVATION ARMY STAFF BAND WITH COMM. REES AND COL. MAIDMENT
AS EMBARKED ON THE ILL-FATED S.S. "EMPRESS OF IRELAND"
THOSE MARKED X WERE RESCUED

OFFICIALS PERISHED.

Several officials of the Phoenix
Bridge Company of Pennsylvania
which was
lost their liv
B. A. Yans
Burke, the
walked out
it collapsed.
John Worle

A very cl
Mr. Ulric
Quebec Brid
of friends fr
who was o
idea of build
out to sho
friends this
scarcely dri
reached the
came, and before they could return to
the edge of the river the whole structure was lying in ruins. A few mo-
ments later and they would have been
killed with the rest.

was the
span, the cantilever arm, and
pended span.
In the House of Commons last ses-

Government would assist the
Bridge Company by becoming its'
banker and lending it money instead
of guaranteeing its bonds.

Mr. Sift
Flelding
was wi
this dias
fied the
er enti
eclarat
was stre
o Gove
 aly for
to ach
ry litt
ange
reof t
ded,
st Lib
r. Bo
ter of
prov
Mr.
ernm
and
Mr
W
case
the
prop
ass
of
tach
ct
t

a solemn their in
gation t
tional c
selves to
I have s
before i
question.
Conservat
but in 18
Conserva
everythin
constitut
in its o
to the m
Sir John
Cartier,
allowance
school ac
the cons
In respec
mitted t
guage of
that occu
said "in
question
sented th
whether,
America
New Br
powers.
He th
upon wh
should in
an exces
the actio
ture migh
of the v
pointing
Brunswic
by the
complish
could be
ed as fo
the Dom
would ha
wrench of
they mi
vince in
control
stitutio

Strategy 20 | Vocabulary

Take notes:
Write down relevant information.

beam n. a long straight heavy piece of wood or metal
crew n. the group of people who work on a ship
pier n. a platform stretching into a river
to plunge v. to fall or move quickly down with a lot of force
to prevent v. to stop something from happening

- Think of an emergency.
- Choose five items you would need in this emergency.

How about candles and matches?

Good idea. I think we need a thermal blanket, too.

You're right. Do we need duct tape?

I don't think so.

AM...

bandages

EMERGENCY SUPPLIES

AM/FM radio
bandages
batteries: AA
batteries: D
blanket: solar
blanket: thermal
booklet of survival strategies
candle
compass
dried food
duct tape
first-aid kit
flares
flashlight
high-energy fruit bars
matches: waterproof
multi-purpose tool
nylon rope
orange caution tape
pencils
plastic bags
red flag
water
whistle

50 GREAT TIPS

b...

...mal

batteries: AA

candles	compass	duct tape	extinguisher

first-aid kit	flares	flashlight: large	flashlight: small

multi-purpose kit	multi-purpose tool	nylon rope
	 (can opener, knife, pliers, scissors, saw blade, screwdriver)	

pencils	survival bag	water	whistle

Strategy 1

Gesture:
Use actions to help transmit your message.

Vocabulary

item *n.* a single article, especially one article in a list
supplies *n.* articles necessary for a particular purpose

ACTIVITY

3 Be Prepared

 15

- Read the information about emergency plans.
- Discuss the emergency plans in your school.

Everyone should be prepared for an emergency. Emergencies can happen to anyone, anywhere and anytime.

ARE YOU READY FOR AN EMERGENCY?

FIRE EMERGENCY PLAN

- Store imflammable materials in a safe place.
- Install smoke detectors on every floor.
- Have a fire extinguisher in the kitchen.
- Remember S.D.R.: Stop. Drop. Roll.
- Plan an escape route from every room.

PERSONAL EMERGENCY PLAN

- Carry identification at all times.
- Carry an emergency telephone number for parents or guardians.
- Carry money for emergency use only.

- Does your family have an emergency evacuation plan?
- Do you have an emergency kit in your home?
- Do you have an emergency kit in the family car?

---

 trategy 18

Scan:
Look or listen for specific information.

 ocabulary

escape route *n.* a way of getting away from a dangerous situation

fire extinguisher *n.* a metal container with water or chemicals in it, used for stopping small fires

kit *n.* a set of tools, equipment etc. for a particular purpose

kitchen *n.* the room where you cook and prepare food

ready *adj.* prepared

smoke *n.* white, grey or black gas produced by something burning

to store *v.* to keep things until you need them

 rammar

GIVING INSTRUCTIONS

We use the imperative to give instructions. The imperative is the base form of the verb: the infinitive without **to**.

For example,
Install fire detectors.
Keep a snow-storm kit in the car.

FINAL CURTAIN

Prepare an emergency response plan.

1 Choose a disaster. For example:
- a fire
- a flood
- a power failure

2 Prepare an emergency response plan. Include a plan of action and an emergency supply kit.

3 Divide the tasks among the members of your team.

Let's divide up the tasks.

O.K. I'll put together an emergency kit. Camille, do you want to help me?

Yes. Let's make a list.

Josh, you and I can prepare the action plan. We can make a poster.

4 Prepare your response plan.

5 Present your plan to your classmates.

The emergency we chose is an ice storm. Camille and I will present the plan of action. Josh and Iohahiio will show you our emergency kit.

6 Consider what you learned during this activity.
- Make a note of new vocabulary.
- Reflect on what you learned about how you and your classmates react to disasters.

 trategies

Remember! Use the strategies you've already practised.
Also try

| Strategy | 3 | **Rephrase:** Use different words to say the same thing. |
| Strategy | 8 | **Recombine:** Try to combine, in a new way, the words and expressions you already know. |

Portfolio

Choose items for your portfolio.

FINAL CURTAIN

Describe a disaster you have experienced.

1 Choose a disaster you have experienced
For example:
- a fire
- a flood
- a power failure

2 Decide on a way to describe the event. For example, you can write:
- a newspaper report
- a poem or song
- a letter

3 Write your account.

> It started to rain on Sunday. The rain froze and the ice was heavy, so power lines collapsed. There was a power failure and schools were closed. Then people left their homes.

4 Consider what you learned during this activity.
- Make a note of new vocabulary.
- Reflect on what you learned about how you and your classmates react to disasters.

Strategies

Remember! Use the strategies you've already practised.
Also try

Strategy 3 **Rephrase:** Use different words to say the same thing.
Strategy 8 **Recombine:** Try to combine, in a new way, the words and expressions you already know.

Portfolio

Choose items for your portfolio.

*All of life is a game,
with rules, defeats
and victories.*
George Best

SPORTS IN THE CLASSROOM

LITERATURE

HISTORY

SOCIAL SCIENCE

MATHMATICS

What can we learn from sports? Sports have always been important to individuals and communities. From ancient times, people have admired athletes. Athletes have been role models for generations of young people. They can teach us about courage, hard work and humility. Playing a sport teaches us about physical fitness, teamwork, the value of practice and the importance of a healthy diet. However, many other things can be learned from sports. Today's athletes must know about mathematics and physics, too. Modern sports fans know more than the rules of the game. Sports and games teach us more than we think.

What can we learn from sports and games?

A. Create a mini-lesson based on a sport.

B. Create an activity based on a sport.

trategy 11	**ocabulary**
Activate prior knowledge: Consider what you already know about the subject.	**fitness** *n.* ability to run or do physical work for a long time **healthy** *adj.* makes you strong and well **fan** *n.* an enthusiastic admirer

 • Listen to the students' conversation.

• Identify the subjects and sports they mention.

SUBJECT	TEACHER	TOPIC	SPORT
	Mrs. Savage	biography	basketball
Science			
Mathematics			

Pay selective attention:
Decide what you should pay attention to before you start your work.

 ocabulary

angle *n.* the space between two straight lines that meet

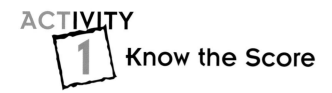

ACTIVITY

1 Know the Score

- Solve the math problems below.
- Write a math problem based on your favourite sport.

1. KNIGHTS 119   BEARS 112   ←   Which team won by more?
   KINGS 101   LIONS 89   How much more?

2. STARS ON ICE

Name	Game 1	Game 2	Game 3	Game 4
Mario	4	5	3	4
Roxanne	4	3	2	5
Kelly	6	5	2	1
John–Thomas	4	4	4	4

← What is each player's average score?

3. Jenna ran five kilometres in four hours. Cynthia ran four kilometres in three hours. Who ran faster?

---

 trategy 26

Take risks:
Experiment and don't be afraid to make mistakes.

 ocabulary

faster *adv.* more rapidly
to win *v.* to come first

---

 rammar

COMPARING QUANTITIES
We use the words **more**, **most**, **less**, **least**, **fewer** and **fewest** to compare quantities.

PLURAL

more (= a larger number)
    The Bears scored **more** goals than the Lions and won the game.

most (= the largest number)
    The Knights won the **most** games and won the tournament.

fewer (= a smaller number)
    The Lions scored **fewer** goals than the Bears and lost the game.

fewest (= the smallest number)
    The Lions won the fewest games and lost the tournament.

UNCOUNTABLE

more (= a larger amount)
    I spend **more** time playing hockey than soccer. I play six hours of hockey and only two hours of soccer.

most (= the largest amount)
    This TV channel shows the **most** hockey. It shows a game every night.

less (= a smaller amount)
    I spend **less** time playing soccer than hockey.

least (= the smallest amount)
    My mother doesn't like hockey. She prefers the TV channel that shows the **least**.

ACTIVITY 2 Historical Greats

- Read about some athletes.
- Decide which of them is a good role model and why.

Athletes are often role models for both young people and adults. A role model is someone people try to be like. This series of cards shows many role models from different sports. Collect them all.

LANCE ARMSTRONG

Born: September 18, 1971
Cyclist
Seven-time winner of the Tour de France

Lance Armstrong's courage has inspired many people. He was diagnosed with cancer after winning the Tour de France bicycle race and fought the disease so that he could continue cycling. In 2005, he won his seventh Tour de France. Lance started a fundraising campaign to support cancer research. Many people wear the yellow Livestrong bracelet. Lance wants people to wear the bracelet until a cure for cancer is found.

JACKIE ROBINSON

Born: January 31, 1919
Died: October 24, 1972
Baseball player
Montréal Royals 1946
Brooklyn Dodgers 1947-1957

Jackie Robinson was the first African-American baseball player to sign a major league contract. He began his career with the Montréal Royals in 1946. Two years later, Robinson was named Most Valuable Player. He had patience and self-control. Some spectators insulted him, some wanted to fight him and others threw things at him. Jackie Robinson's playing and patience earned him the respect of his teammates and his fans.

MAMIE "PEANUT" JOHNSON

Born: September 27, 1935
Baseball player
Indianapolis Clowns 1953-1955

Mamie Johnson had a dream. She wanted to be a professional baseball pitcher. She also had determination, courage and a fierce curveball. She finally realized her dream. She joined the Indianapolis Clowns of the Negro League, the American Baseball League for African-Americans only, and pitched professionally for three years. She was one of only three women to play on a professional men's team.

Strategy 6

Direct attention:
Focus your attention.
Don't be distracted.

Vocabulary

disease *n.* an illness
fundraising *adj.* collecting money for a specific purpose
to pitch *v.* to throw a ball to a batter
self-control *n.* ability to manage your actions and emotions
to throw *v.* to send through the air with force

3 Sports and Language: Three Strikes and You're Out

- Find the sports expressions in the texts below.
- Add more expressions to the list.

Skatepark Plan on Target

Lemmingway's mayor announced yesterday that the plans for a new skatepark are on target. Last year the local council scored points with high school students when they announced the game plan. Mr. Winterton said that city streets would be out of bounds to skateboarders once the park was put into play.

High School Musical a Hit!

Students at Lemmingway High School scored a big hit last night. Parents and teachers agreed that the concert was on a par with a professional performance. Students had a slam dunk with their songs. The audience shouted their praise as they swung into the final number. Everyone agreed that it was a major league performance.

EXPRESSION	MEANING	RELATED SPORT
Ace	Get a perfect score	tennis
Get a head start	Begin before others	racing
Go overboard	Do too much, exaggerate	sailing, boating
Make the cut	Be selected for something	all sports
Off base	Incorrect	baseball
Play ball	Cooperate	baseball

Hey Josh, I aced that test. How did you do?

I was way off base. I only got 65%.

S trategy 3

Rephrase:
Use different words to say the same thing.

FINAL CURTAIN

Create a mini-lesson based on a sport.

1 With your partners, choose a sport.

2 Think of a way that your sport can be used in a school subject: for example, math, history, language.

3 Research this aspect of the sport you have chosen.

4 Assign roles and responsibilities to each member of your team.

5 Decide how to present your ideas.

6 Write up your presentation.

7 Share your ideas with your classmates.

> We chose basketball.

> Our subjects are history and mathematics.

> In history we learned the story of the Toronto Raptors.

> In math, we presented statistics for Michael Jordan and Wilt Chamberlain.

SUBJECT	LEARN ABOUT	QUESTION/TASK
History	The Toronto Raptors Statistics for Jordan and Chamberlain	Write a timeline.
Mathematics		Who is better?

Strategies

Remember! Use the strategies you've already practised.
Also try

Strategy 2 **Recast:** Check if you understand someone by repeating what she or he says.
Strategy 23 **Cooperate:** Work with others to achieve a goal.

Portfolio

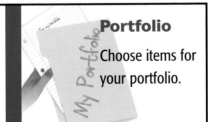

Choose items for your portfolio.

FINAL CURTAIN

Create an activity based on a sport.

Option **B**

1 Choose a sport.

2 Decide on a subject that can include your sport: for example, math, history, language.

3 Write an activity.

4 Present your activity to your classmates.

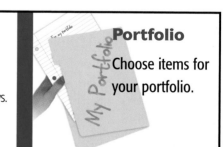

SPORTS

1. In soccer, players score goals.

2. In tennis, players hit a ball over a net.

---

trategies

Remember! Use the strategies you've already practised.
Also try

Strategy 2   **Recast:** Check if you understand someone by repeating what she or he says.
Strategy 23 **Cooperate:** Work with others to achieve a goal.

Portfolio

Choose items for your portfolio.

My Portfolio

Boys will be boys. And even that wouldn't matter if only we could prevent girls from being girls.

Anthony Hope

BOYS AND GIRLS: SAME BUT DIFFERENT?

"It's not fair. He can stay out later just because he's a boy."

"She never gets in trouble. It's because she's a girl."

Have you ever thought or said something like this? Are you ever treated differently just because you are a boy or a girl? Maybe your parents treat you differently from your brother or sister. At school, you might think that your teachers expect different things from boys and girls. Let's face it—at school or at home, in your free-time and social activities, boys and girls aren't always the same! Listening to each other and learning about your differences can help you understand each other better.

What do you have to say about boys and girls?

A. Play "He Says, She Says."

B. Write a letter to a teen magazine.

UNIT 9

---

 trategy 11

Activate prior knowledge:
Consider what you already know about the subject.

V **ocabulary**

to expect *v.* to demand, to want

SETTING THE SCENE

- Think about some of the differences between boys and girls in school, with friends, with families and in free-time activities.

 Complete the prompts.

Girls are/like/don't like/want/ etc. . . .

Boys are/like/don't like/want/etc. . . .

- Share your ideas to make a class list of boy-girl characteristics.

 Quick Writes: Keeping it quick!

- Write in your response journal.

- Don't worry about spelling or grammar.

- If you can't think of a word, draw a picture or use other words to describe what you mean.

- If you get stuck writing a sentence, note down key words.

- Try not to stop writing. Don't stop your ideas from flowing.

- Write as much as you can until your teacher tells you to stop.

 Play computer games, like fashion, good at math

 are fun, like shopping, don't like dancing

---

trategy 5	ocabulary
Substitute: When you don't know the word for something, try to describe it.	**to flow** v. to move along in a steady way, like water **to be stuck** v. to be unable to continue because something is too difficult **to worry** v. to be anxious

ACTIVITY

1 Boys Will Be Boys

- Think of your favourite character in a television show, book or movie.
- List the character's personality traits, strengths and weaknesses.
- Present the information to a partner. Don't tell your partner who the character is.
- Ask your partner to decide if the character is male or female and to explain his or her choice.

determined
powerful
independent

My character is from a television show. This person is determined, powerful and independent.

So, what do you think?
Is my character male or female?

I'm not sure. I think it's probably a man, because in television shows men are often more powerful and independent than women.

- Are adults' expectations of boys and girls influenced by the media?

 trategy 22

Ask for help, repetition, clarification, confirmation:
Request assistance.

 ocabulary

powerful *adj.* strong
strength *n.* a positive quality
weakness *n.* a negative quality

ACTIVITY 2 Picking Your Brain

Before you read

Think about your experiences in school from kindergarten until now.

- What do you remember about boys and girls in your classes? For example, who took the best notes? Who had the best marks? Who used the computer more often? Who were the most active? The most imaginative? The strongest leaders?

 trategy 18

Scan:
Look or listen for specific information.

 ocabulary

brain *n.* the organ inside your head that controls how you think, feel and move
to be inclined *v.* to have a tendency

 rammar

COMPARING TWO ACTIONS

To compare two actions, use the words
more or **less** + adverb + **than**.

Jen asks questions **more often than** Jeremy does.
Jen can concentrate **more easily than** Jeremy can.
Jeremy does his work **less carefully than** Jen does.

There are exceptions.
Jeremy can run faster **than** Jen can.
Jen can sing **well**, but Jeremy can sing **better than** Jen.

rammar

COMPARING TWO PEOPLE OR THINGS

To compare two things, add the suffix **er** to the adjective and use the word **than**.

Jeremy is tall**er** than Jen.
Jen is quiet**er than** Jeremy.

For some two-syllable adjectives and all adjectives that have three or more syllables, use the words **more** or **less** + **than**.

Jen is **more careful than** Jeremy.
Jeremy is **less attentive than** Jen.

Some spelling rules:
For one-syllable words that have a consonant-vowel-consonant pattern, double the final consonant and add **er**.

big	big**ger**
hot	hot**ter**

For two-syllable adjectives ending in **y**, change the **y** to **i** and add **er**.

eas**y**	eas**ier**
happ**y**	happ**ier**

Don't forget the irregulars.

good	better
bad	worse

While you read

- Read the text.
- Take notes while you read.
- Find five differences between boys and girls.

Do the girls in your class seem to work harder than the boys? Does it seem that the boys dominate in some subjects? Do the girls often finish reading first?

You probably answered yes, yes and yes.

Research has shown that girls are generally more interested in school life than boys. They believe success at school will help them in their adult life, and they make more effort even in subjects they are not interested in. They also spend more time on homework and studying than boys. Boys often find it difficult to make an effort if they don't see the immediate benefits. Many boys admire other boys who get good marks only if they seem to get them without studying.

Boys and girls generally learn differently, too. Most boys like to learn a subject by understanding it and finding the connections between the different parts. Girls are more inclined to learn by repeating and memorizing their work. Girls are usually better at planning, organizing and structuring their work. They like to work in groups and to help and support each other. Boys are more competitive with each other.

Girls have an easier time learning to read and write and then continue to read more than boys. This helps them with their school work because reading and writing are an important part of every subject. Girls are inclined to have a higher opinion of their abilities than boys, too, which helps them to achieve good results.

Boys generally have more energy than girls. They find it more difficult to sit still and concentrate for long periods of time. They need to be active and are inclined to dominate the classroom and get more attention than girls.

Some research suggests that there are differences in the male and female brains that may explain why boys and girls act the way they do. But there are other influences, too. Some attitudes we learn from our parents, role models and the people around us. Besides, all girls are not the same and neither are all boys. Just look around you.

After you read

What did you find the most interesting in this text? What do you agree or disagree with?

- Share your ideas with a partner.

3 Together or Apart

Before you listen

Have you ever been in an all-boy or all-girl class? If so, what did you think of it? Would you prefer to be in a class like this for any of your subjects? Which ones? Why or why not?

🎧 • Listen to the teacher and students.

• Answer the questions.

1. What subject does Michèle teach?
2. How does she describe the boys in her all-boy group?
3. Did the boys' math results change? If so, how?
4. In which subjects did Charles have all-boy classes?
5. In which class did it make a difference? Why?
6. What was one good thing about Ivanie's all-girl class?
7. What was one bad thing?
8. What does Ivanie say about working in teams?

• Write down which each person preferred, separate groups or mixed groups.

• Give one reason for each person's choice.

• Decide if you would like to be in all-girl or all-boy classes.

• Share your opinion with the class.

• Find out what your classmates think.

I loved teaching the boys. They were active and full of energy.

The good thing was that I worked harder, but the bad thing was that the class wasn't as much fun.

It made a difference in phys. ed. class.

trategy 7

Pay selective attention:
Decide what you should pay attention to before you start your work.

ACTIVITY 4 On the Weekend

- Write down your typical weekend activities.

Friday	Saturday	Sunday
SCHOOL	Morning: – diving lessons – shopping	Morning: – watch TV – relax – read
Lunch	Lunch	Lunch
SCHOOL	Afternoon: – chat – play soccer – do homework	Afternoon: – visit family
Supper	Supper	Supper
Evening: – go to movie with friends	Evening: – watch movie with friends	Evening: – do homework

trategy 12

Compare:
Note the similarities and differences
between two or more things.

- Compare your information with a girl and with a boy.
- Note down your similarities and differences.
- Use a different colour to represent the girl's answers and the boy's answers.
- Decide if you have more in common with the boy or the girl.

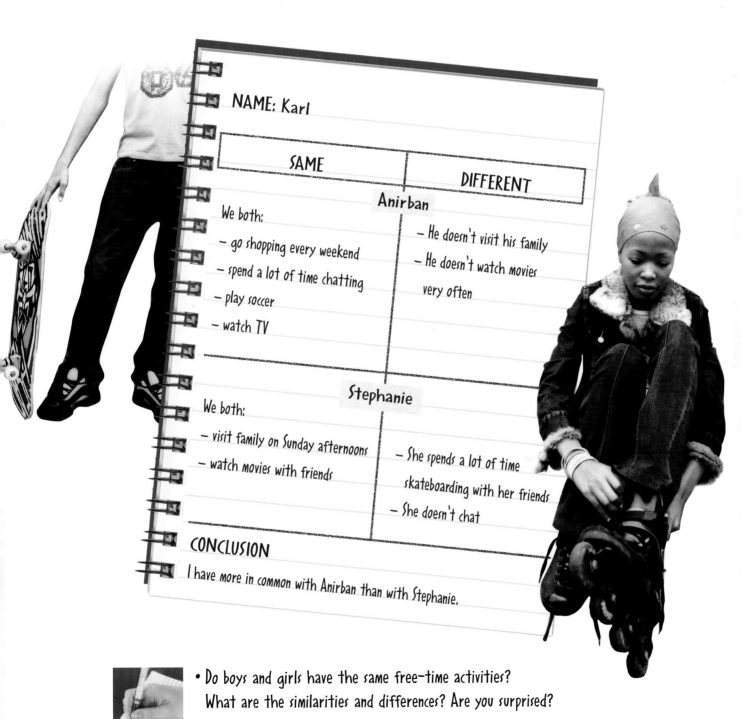

NAME: Karl

SAME	DIFFERENT
Anirban	
We both:	
– go shopping every weekend	– He doesn't visit his family
– spend a lot of time chatting	– He doesn't watch movies
– play soccer	very often
– watch TV	
Stephanie	
We both:	
– visit family on Sunday afternoons	– She spends a lot of time
– watch movies with friends	skateboarding with her friends
	– She doesn't chat

CONCLUSION

I have more in common with Anirban than with Stephanie.

- Do boys and girls have the same free-time activities?
  What are the similarities and differences? Are you surprised?

ACTIVITY

5 Point of View

- With a partner of the same sex as you, think of something you would like to find out about the opposite sex.

- Write a guiding question.

> Are boys and girls equally interested in music?

What do you think you will find out?
Predict what the answer to your question will be.

- Write five interview questions.
- Pair up with two other students.
- Interview each other.
- Compare your answers.

Question	Damien	Nick
1. What kind of music do you like most?	Pop music.	Lots of stuff. Rock and hip-hop mainly.
2. How important is music to you?	Quite important.	Very important.
3. How long do you spend listening to music each day?	About an hour.	At least three h It varies.

What did you learn from this activity?
Were your predictions correct?
Are you surprised by the results?
Why or why not?

trategy 23

Cooperate:
Work with others to achieve a goal.

FINAL CURTAIN

Play "He Says, She Says."

RULES OF THE GAME

- You must listen carefully to each other.
- You must pay attention to your partners and respect each other's opinions.
- You must participate in the game. Each person on the team must speak at least once.
- Your team will get one point for each well-justified opinion. You will get an extra point if you are the first ones to answer.
- You have to justify your opinion.

1 Form a team of four boys or four girls.

2 Listen to the statements your teacher reads to you.

> "Boys play more computer games than girls."
> He says . . .

3
- Think about the statement and form your opinion. You have one minute.
- Use the information in the unit, your response journal and what you already know about boys and girls.
- Compare your ideas with those of your teammates.

We, boys and girls, agree that
1. Boys play more computer games than girls.
2.

> We agree too, because . . .

> We agree, because . . .

4 Decide what the team's opinion is.

What did you learn about boys and girls in this unit? Did your opinion change?

Strategies

Remember! Use the strategies you've already practised.
Also try

Strategy 10 Self-monitor: Check and correct your work.

Portfolio

Choose items for your portfolio.

My Portfolio

Write a letter to a magazine to give your views about boys and girls.

1
- Read the cards your teacher gives you.
- Choose a statement which you agree or disagree with.

Note down the reasons for your opinion. You could use
- an idea web
- a brainstorming list

2

Boys need more rules than girls.

> **Boys need more rules than girls.**
> I disagree because:
> – rules are for everybody (1)
> – if boys get into more trouble it's because they're not obeying the rules
> – if boys disobey rules more than girls – why? (3)
> – boys and girls should get the same punishment (2)

3
Write a letter to a teen magazine. Give your opinion on the statement and explain your reasons.

> Dear Teen Magazine:
>
> I don't agree that boys need more rules than girls. Rules are for everybody. If somebody disobeys a rule, they should receive a punishment. It shouldn't be different if they're a girl or a boy. If boys disobey the rules more than girls, we should find out why.
>
> Chris

What did you learn about boys and girls in this unit? Did your opinion change?

Strategies

Remember! Use the strategies you've already practised. Also try

Strategy 10   Self-monitor: Check and correct your work.

Portfolio

Choose items for your portfolio.

My Portfolio

*Every exit is an entrance
somewhere else.*
Tom Stoppard

MAKING HEADLINES

This year, you took centre stage. It's almost time for you to exit the stage and move on to the next act. Before you go, think about what you have accomplished so far. This is your chance to go from centre stage to the front page!

Why are you making the headlines?

UNIT 10

A. Put your class on the front page.

B. Write headlines about the year's special events.

Strategy 11

Activate prior knowledge:
Consider what you already know about the subject.

Vocabulary

front page *n.* first page

SETTING THE SCENE

- See how many of the following elements you can find on the front page of a newspaper.
- Write the information in your notebook.

1. Title   The Lemmingway Gazette

2. Date   March 12, 2007

TITLE

DATE

HEADLINE

INDEX

TODAY'S WEATHER

ARTICLE

Teen Zone wins provincial grant to build swimming pool. Mayor congratulates teens on hard work. A3

THE LEMMINGWAY GAZETTE

Lemmingway • Saturday, March 12, 2007 • lemmingwaygazette.com • First edition

WEB SITE

EDITION

TAKING CENTRE STAGE

Local teens win prestigious modelling contract

Several teens from the Lemmingway area have been chosen to represent Quebec youth in a new ESL textbook. Story and photos in *Saturday Plus*, D2

PHOTO

INDEX	
AngloFiles	C4
Books	C4
Business	B1
Classified	B5
Comics	D6
Editorials	A2
Lifestyle	D1
Sports	E1
Travel	F1

WEATHER

CLOUDY WITH SNOW
High -3°
Low -10°

FIRE IN LOCAL HIGH SCHOOL DESTROYS SCIENCE LAB

Carl Woodward

Firefighters battled to save the science lab at Lemmingway High last night. They were called out when a neighbour noticed smoke and flames coming from a top-floor window. By the time the fire brigade arrived, fire had engulfed the building. After three hours, firefighters managed to extinguish the fire but the science lab was completely destroyed. Police chief June Austen said that foul play was not suspected. "Our students will be devastated," said school principal Norman Chomsky. "They were very proud of the lab."

For more, see A7

BUY THE NEW TEEN MAG EVERYONE'S TALKING ABOUT.

QUIZ ME! on newsstands now
Only $1.75

ADVERTISEMENT

trategy 20
Take notes:
Write down relevant information.

11 18

- Look at the cover page of each unit in *Centre Stage 2*.
- Review the stories and projects.
- Choose the activity that you liked the best this year and explain why.

What was your favourite activity this year?

I'm not sure. I definitely liked doing the projects better than reading the stories.

Not me. I preferred the stories. I was very proud of myself because I understood most of them.

Is that what you're going to choose as your favourite activity?

No, not necessarily. I'd rather choose a final-curtain activity. I think I'll go with the character card I created for the Contami-Nation game. I really used my imagination for that one. My illustration turned out really well.

That's a good idea. I'm going to choose the adults' guide for teenagers. That was a great activity. I actually gave it to my parents and it helped us communicate more.

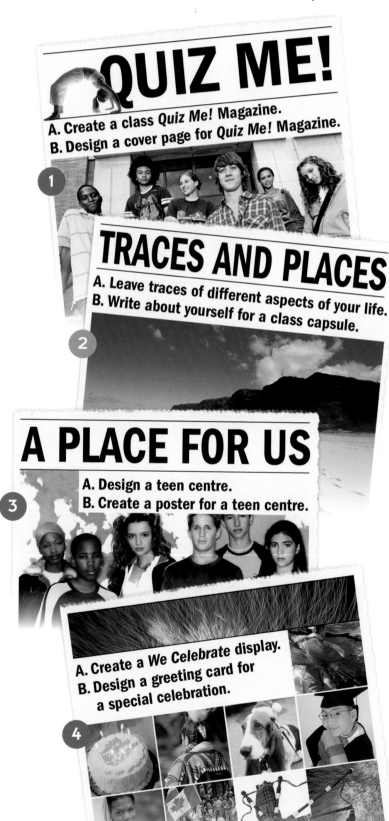

QUIZ ME!
A. Create a class *Quiz Me!* Magazine.
B. Design a cover page for *Quiz Me!* Magazine.
1

TRACES AND PLACES
A. Leave traces of different aspects of your life.
B. Write about yourself for a class capsule.
2

A PLACE FOR US
A. Design a teen centre.
B. Create a poster for a teen centre.
3

A. Create a We Celebrate display.
B. Design a greeting card for a special celebration.
4

DO YOU SPEAK ADULT?

A. Write a communication guide for parents and other adults.
B. Write a postcard to your parent or another adult.

5

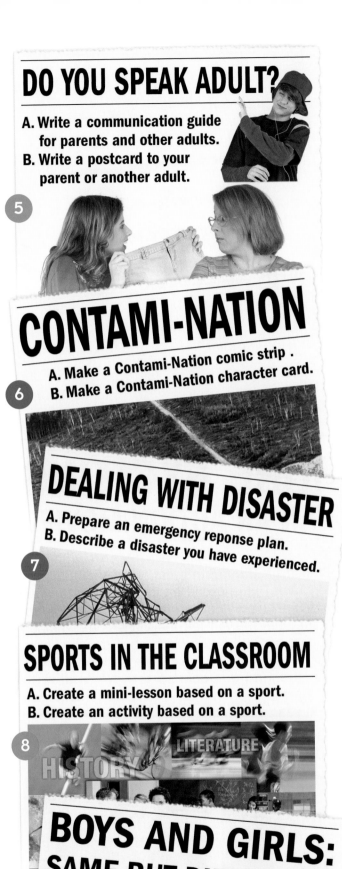

CONTAMI-NATION

A. Make a Contami-Nation comic strip .
B. Make a Contami-Nation character card.

6

DEALING WITH DISASTER

A. Prepare an emergency reponse plan.
B. Describe a disaster you have experienced.

7

SPORTS IN THE CLASSROOM

A. Create a mini-lesson based on a sport.
B. Create an activity based on a sport.

8

BOYS AND GIRLS: SAME BUT DIFFERENT?

9

A. Play "He Says, She Says."
B. Write a letter to a teen magazine.

THE STORIES

1. Cyberpirates

2. Into Thin Air

3. A Cold, Dark Night

4. Another Kind of Hero

THE PROJECTS

1. From High Seas to Cyberspace

2. Passion for Fashion

3. Teens on Air

*g*rammar

TALKING ABOUT PAST EVENTS

We use the simple past tense to express past time. To form the past tense of most verbs, add **d** or **ed** to the base form.

I think I'll go with the character card I creat**ed** for the Contami-Nation game. I really us**ed** my imagination for that one. My illustration turn**ed** out very well.

Some verbs have an irregular past tense form. See the reference section for a list.

That **was** a great activity. I **gave** the guide to my parents.

*S*trategy 22

Skim:
Read through a text quickly to get a general overview.

*V*ocabulary

to turn out *v.* to have a particular result

ACTIVITY 2 Front Page Fever

- Read the news article below and find the following:
  - surprising or attention-catching information in the opening sentence
  - three action words
  - the answers *who*, *what*, *when*, *where*, *why*, *how*
  - a quotation which states an opinion
  - two catchy expressions in the concluding sentence

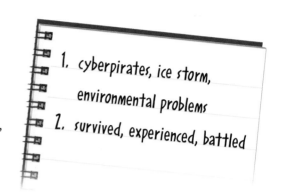

1. cyberpirates, ice storm, environmental problems
2. survived, experienced, battled

Centre Stage

SCHOOL: MORE EXCITING THAN AN ACTION MOVIE?

Dan Wood

Students in Group 8 this year survived an attack by cyberpirates, experienced an ice storm and battled environmental problems using superhuman powers. And they never even left the classroom! Through activities in their English class, they travelled from the past to the present and even started thinking about the future. Because they were able to participate in a variety of activities, the students had a great year.

These students certainly took centre stage and now they're making headlines!

"Every class was a new adventure," said student Marco De Luca. "I really loved learning about the different disasters. This is one class that wasn't a disaster for me!"

"It was a great year," added Cassandra Karnis, excitedly. "I've never had so much fun in English class before."

"I liked reading all the stories," said Amanda Derix, "but I particularly loved the one about cyberpirates."

WRITING AN EFFECTIVE NEWSPAPER ARTICLE

- Grab your readers' attention by writing something that will surprise them, shock them or make them laugh. You can also start with a question or a direct quotation. Give the most interesting information first. You want to hook your readers!

- Use active words to help your readers feel that they are part of the action.

- Provide the following information: *who*, *what*, *when*, *where*, *why*, *how*.

- Be objective and write in the third person (*he*, *she*, *it*, *they*). Don't give your personal opinion: just state the facts. You can use quotations to indicate other people's opinions.

- Conclude your article with a strong statement, a catchy phrase or a direct quotation.

- Write some questions to ask your partner. For example:
  - What was your favourite activity, unit, story or project?
  - Why was this your favourite?
  - What did you learn from it?
  - When did you do it?
  - How would you describe your experience in English class this year?
- Interview your partner and and note down his or her answers.
- Read the tips on the left.
- Write a newspaper article about your partner.

 trategy 18

Plan:
Think about what you need to do to achieve a goal.

 ocabulary

to battle *v.* to fight
to hook *v.* to attract and keep
to pay off *v.* to have a good result
really *adv.* very
to shock *v.* to surprise and upset

 rammar

QUOTING SOMEONE'S WORDS

A direct quotation is the use of someone else's exact words in your own writing. There is a quotation on the cover page of each unit in this book.

When you incorporate a direct quotation into your own writing, there are some rules to follow.

Use quotation marks around the direct quotation.
> "Every class was a new adventure," said student Marco De Luca.

Use a capital letter for the first word of a direct quotation.
> Ms. Salmaso said, "The students worked really hard."

Use a comma to introduce a quotation.
> Ms. Salmaso said, "Their hard work paid off."

If the direct quotation is divided, don't use a capital letter for the second part of the quotation.
> "I liked reading all the stories," said Amanda Derix, "but I particularly loved the one about cyberpirates."

Place punctuation like commas and periods inside the quotations marks.
> "It was a great year," added Cassandra Karnis, excitedly. "I've never had so much fun in English class before."

ACTIVITY 3 Heads-Up Headlines

- Look at some newspapers.
- Find three headlines that catch your attention and explain why you find them interesting.
- Read the tips on the right.
- Read the headlines below.
- Decide which capitalization rules are used.
- Identify the type of headline: a question, a well-known expression or a statement.
- Write a headline for your news article.

> - Group 1 Leaves Traces for the Future
> - statement
> - capitalize first letter of important words

Group 1 Leaves Traces for the Future

Sarah B. Solves Cybercrime

Students in Group 14 Study the Gender Gap

Ms. Salmaso's students take centre stage

School: more exciting than an action movie?

TIPS

WRITING EFFECTIVE HEADLINES

Often people don't have time to read a newspaper from cover to cover. Headlines help people determine which articles they'll read. The headlines must therefore catch the readers' attention.

- You can:
  - ask a question
  - use a well-known expression
  - make a statement

- Here are some capitalization rules to keep in mind. Capitalize the first word and proper nouns (names of people and places). Capitalize the first letter of all important words. See the capitalization rules for titles in the reference section.

trategy 16

Predict:
Make a hypothesis based on the information you already have.

FINAL CURTAIN

Put your class on the front page.

1 Finalize your news article.

2 Revise and edit it. Make sure it is ready to be published.

3 Check your headline again. You can cut out letters and words from newspapers to create your own headline.

4 Present your news article to your partner.

GROUP 3 GOES TO TORONTO

5 Put your headline on the front page.

---

 trategies

Remember! Use the strategies you've already practised.
Also try

Strategy 10 **Self monitor:** Check and correct your work.
Strategy 23 **Cooperate:** Work with others to achieve a goal.

Portfolio

Choose items for your portfolio.

FINAL CURTAIN

Write headlines about the year's special events.

Option B

1 Make a list of five important events that happened in the past year.

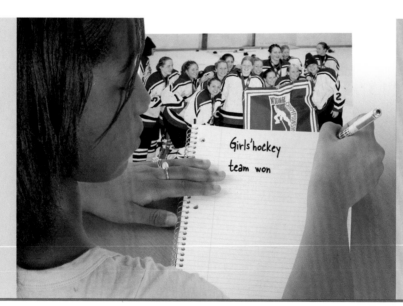

Girls' hockey team won

2 Write a headline for each event.

3 Display your headlines in the classroom.

Strategies

Remember! Use the strategies you've already practised. Also try

Strategy 10 **Self monitor:** Check and correct your work.
Strategy 23 **Cooperate:** Work with others to achieve a goal.

Portfolio

Choose items for your portfolio.

My Portfolio

STORIES

CYBERPIRATES

Before You Read

• Answer the questions on the screen.

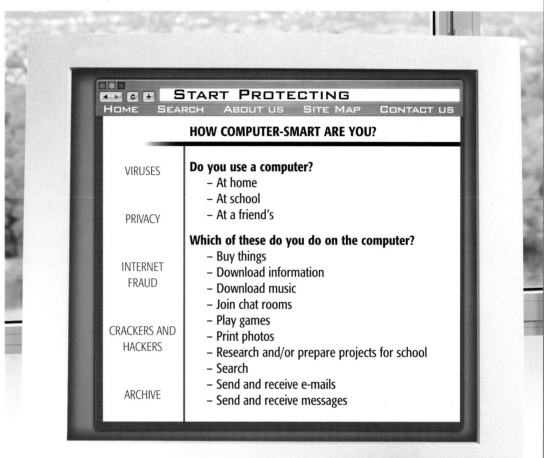

START PROTECTING

Home   Search   About us   Site Map   Contact us

HOW COMPUTER-SMART ARE YOU?

VIRUSES

PRIVACY

INTERNET
FRAUD

CRACKERS AND
HACKERS

ARCHIVE

Do you use a computer?
– At home
– At school
– At a friend's

Which of these do you do on the computer?
– Buy things
– Download information
– Download music
– Join chat rooms
– Play games
– Print photos
– Research and/or prepare projects for school
– Search
– Send and receive e-mails
– Send and receive messages

When You Read

• Create a cyberspace dictionary.

• Start with these words:
  – chat room
  – cracker

• Think about the question(s)
  at the bottom of the pages.

Cracker:
someone who breaks
into a computer to
steal information
(criminal hacker)

trategy 11

Activiate prior knowledge:
Consider what you already
know about the subject.

O.K. That's it. We've finished. Let's e-mail the guys and tell them we can hand in our project.

All right! I think we did a great job.

That's it. It looks great.

Yeah. Let's e-mail it to Sheila and Val right away.

All right, but let's go over to Val's house. She has a super colour printer. I want to see what the project looks like in colour.

• What are the students doing on their computers?

I just got your part of the project. I put the parts together and now I'm sending it to school.

What on earth! What's this?

Ahoy there!
Captain Kidd has come aboard your computer.

- What problem do the students encounter?

What happened to our stuff? Where'd it go?

Val! What did you do?

She didn't **do** anything. It just vanished.

Don't panic and don't touch any keys. Sheila, call Tapper John.

Tapper John? Who's that?

He is just a computer geek, a computer genius. He goes to our school. And he's my cousin.

- Whom do the students ask for help?

Hello.

Hi, John. It's Sheila.

Hey, Sheila, what's up?

I'm working on a project with some classmates and we have a problem.

Like what?

A message flashed on the screen and then our project document disappeared.

What did the message say?

"Ahoy there! Captain Kidd has come aboard your computer."

Oh, Captain Kidd! He's a cracker.

A what? Wait, wait, I'm putting you on the speaker.

A cracker's someone who gets into other people's computers and takes their stuff. No one knows who Captain Kidd is. He or she is an expert cracker, for sure.

Why take our project?

To sell it to other students. That's the business. This cracker finds projects and compositions and other school work and sells them to students.

That's got to be illegal.

Sure is. Did you save the work on your hard drive or make a backup copy? If you did, it isn't lost. You should have a firewall on your machine, Sheila.

I do. But we were using my friend's computer.

That's too bad. I'm afraid it's gone. Sorry I can't help.

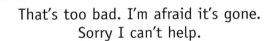

Oh no! Well, thanks anyway. Bye.

- Who caused the problem?
- What do the students find out about this person?

Well, it's gone.
All our work's been stolen.

What are we going to do now?

Hold on. I think kids
at school should be warned
about this cracker thing.

That's it! That's our new project.
We'll warn everyone about cybercrime.

Great idea! It's modern piracy.
What's everyone going to do?

Well, I could make
some posters.

Val, you write well.
How about writing
an article for the
school newspaper?

Sure. I can do that.

I'll set up a Web page about things to do to protect your documents. Tapper John can help me.

I'll record a warning for the school intercom.

I never thought a cracker would hit my computer.

I guess crackers really are modern-day pirates.

Well, we can fight back!

- What do the students decide to do?
- What is each person's task?

After You Read

• Answer the following questions.

1. The characters decide to take action against cyberpirates. Which action do you think will be most useful? Why?
2. What did you learn about computers from this story?
3. Do you have computers in your school? At home? What kind?
4. How are they protected from cyberpiracy?
5. Do you know anyone like Tapper John?
6. Which of the characters from the story would you like to meet, if any?
7. What makes this story realistic?

• Write some guidelines for protecting computers from cybercrime.

1. I think the Web site will be useful. The students can update it.

1. Never reveal your password.
2. Install a firewall

𝒱ocabulary

backup *n.* a copy of a computer document, program etc, which is made in case the original becomes lost or damaged

cyber *prefix* relating to computers, especially to messages and information on the Internet

illegal *adj.* against the law

to vanish *v.* to disappear

to warn *v.* to tell someone that something bad or dangerous may happen, so that she or he can avoid it or prevent it

BACKGROUND

There are many kinds of cybercrime. Some cybercriminals steal other peoples' identities, personal information and bank account numbers. Others send pornographic messages and images to people's e-mail addresses, or release viruses that destroy data. A cyberpirate can shut down an airport or block a telephone network with a single virus. Cybercriminals also use the Internet for illegal gambling and financial dealings.

Cybercrime is growing as use of the Internet grows. Police all over the world have special officers to fight cybercrime. Large companies hire specialists to protect their systems.

Some cyberpirates are young adults, even teens. They enjoy the challenge of breaking into other people's computers. Sometimes their success ends with a conviction for cybercrime.

How can you beat cybercrime?

INTO THIN AIR

Before You Read

- Think of three words related to doing problem-solving projects.
- Write them down.

When You Read

- Think about the question(s) at the bottom of the pages.

Look at the illustrations. What do you think the story is about?

trategy 16

Predict:
Make a hypothesis based on the information you already have.

Where Am I?
To solve the problem, search and soon you'll see. Initially, the clues all lead to me.

Four students stood at the door of Ms. Ohm's classroom. It was late afternoon. The students had to do some extra work. They looked at the empty room. Ms. Ohm was the social science teacher and she was always on time. She was never late for anything. This was strange. The message on the board was even stranger.

- Why are the students in Ms. Ohm's classroom?
- What does Ms. Ohm teach?
- Ms. Ohm isn't there. Why do the students find this strange?

lead to me.

Julie stepped into the class and went directly to the desk. The others followed. Julie pointed to the envelope on the desk.

Sebastian reacted first. "Lazy! What did we do? She must be upset with us." He was always thinking about other people's feelings.

"Why?" asked Chloe, who needed a reason for everything.

Chloe opened the envelope and the four read the note. It didn't make sense.

Julie was the first to speak. "O.K. This must be a riddle or something."

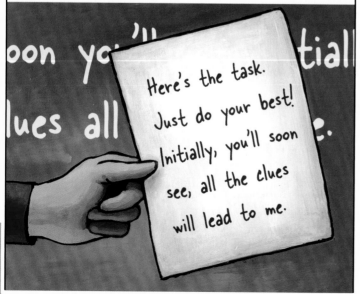

oon yo'll tial

lues all

Here's the task. Just do your best! Initially, you'll soon see, all the clues will lead to me.

Julie, Kazu, Sebastian and Chloe read the letter again and again. Then Sebastian said, "Right, she wants to challenge us. Get it? She thinks we haven't been using our brains. We've been working on problem-solving. This is a problem. We have to solve it."

They thought for a moment and then agreed. It was just the kind of an unusual assignment Ms. Ohm liked to give.

"O.K. Where do we start?" asked Kazu.

"Right here." Chloe pointed to the desk. "Anything unusual will be a clue."

Sebastian noticed something unusual. There was a cup of tea and a ham and egg sandwich on the desk. "Look. Ms. Ohm is allergic to eggs and she's a vegetarian. And she only drinks coffee."

- Who thinks Ms. Ohm is upset? Why?
- What kind of assignment does Ms. Ohm give the students?
- What does Chloe say they should look for?

"Yeah, Kazu, maybe the flowers are a clue too. Are they really marigolds?" Chloe asked.

"Sure," said Kazu. He knew everything about plants. So Julia wrote *marigolds* on her list.

"How do you know that?" asked Chloe."

"I notice things about people," Sebastian replied.

"I'll make a list of what we think are clues," said Julia. Julia was always writing things down. She wrote *tea*, *ham*, *egg*.

"Yuck! Get out of there," Sebastian called to Kazu, who was emptying the wastebasket.

"No, there are always clues in wastebaskets," Kazu answered. "Look. I found a pair of glasses."

"Ms. Ohm doesn't wear glasses," said Julie. "Even I noticed that."

Kazu held up a page. "What's that?" asked Sebastian.

"It's a page from a sailing magazine," said Kazu. "Look. It's a yacht, and I bet it's a clue, too."

Julia wrote *glasses* and *yacht* on her list.

Chloe suggested that they look around the class for other clues.

Kazu pointed to some flowers. "Marigolds," he said. "Does she like marigolds?"

"I don't know," said Sebastian. "I don't know everything about her, you know."

"Well, those flowers weren't there yesterday," Kazu replied.

- What does Kazu find in the wastebasket?
- What kind of flowers does Ms. Ohm like?

They continued to search. It was a strange puzzle and they were uncertain about what they were doing. Sebastian reassured them. "We can do this. We can. We'll solve this."

Julia smiled. She handed her list to Chloe and said, "Look at this list. Look carefully. Do you see what I see?" Chloe nodded. She pointed to the list and said, "This and this and this."

"Yes," said Julie. "There's a pattern. We solved the puzzle!"

Julie ran out of the classroom and down the hall. The others followed her. She pushed open the doors at the end of the hall. They rushed in.

Ms. Ohm was waiting for them. She looked at her watch and smiled. "Ah, you did it. Good job!"

"Now let me explain this special test," Ms. Ohm continued. She explained that each of them had a special and unique talent. The task showed them what these talents were and how they could use them to help one another. "You'll be a team this year," she said. "I hope you can use what you've learned to do all your projects."

Kazu looked puzzled. "I don't get it."

Julie put her hand on Kazu's shoulder. "Let me help you with that," she said.

- Who solves the problem?
- What word is the first clue?

After You Read

- Think of the clues the students gathered.
- Solve the problem with your partner.

Were your predictions correct?

What are the students' special talents?
What are YOUR special talents?

ocabulary

challenge *n.* something that tests strength or ability
clue *n.* an object or a piece of information that helps someone solve a crime or mystery
lazy *adj.* not liking to do work
strange *adj.* unusual or surprising

BACKGROUND

Everyone has a unique and special talent. Some people are exceptional musicians, like Glenn Gould or Céline Dion. Some are superb athletes, like Cindy Klassen. Others are wonderful with words, like Margaret Atwood. Still others may be amazing with numbers or able to create gardens or paint beautiful paintings. They may understand and work with people in unique and helpful ways.

Dr. Howard Gardner of Harvard University has suggested that the traditional idea of intelligence is too limited and does not account for genius in areas such as sports and art. He has identified eight kinds of intelligence and believes that people are word smart, number smart, picture smart, body smart, music smart, people smart, self smart or nature smart.

What kind of smart are you?

A COLD, DARK NIGHT

Before You Read

- Rate the following situations.

1 = very scary
2 = scary
3 = a little scary
4 = not scary

1. You are alone late at night and the lights go out.
2. You are in a dark forest at night.
3. You hear a loud scream at night.
4. Suddenly everything goes silent.
5. You hear a voice but no one is nearby.

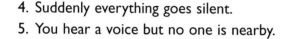

Situation	Rating
1	
2	2
3	

When You Read

- Write down the important words in each scene.

- Think about the question(s) at the bottom of the pages.

Scene 1
two kids, old man, forest,
Grover's Grave

Scene 2

trategy 17

Recombine:
Try to combine, in a new way, the words and expressions you already know.

Uncle Amos, why do they call our forest Grover's Grave?

Was it always called that?

Scene 2

"No, no," said Amos. "They started calling it Grover's Grave after what happened many many years ago. I was just a boy. I was about your age.

"Yes, I remember it well. It was a cold, dark night in October. The snow was like a thin, quiet blanket on the ground. My hands were as cold as ice. I walked into Grover Forest with Amber. Amber was a beautiful big, golden dog."

Scene 3

"Were you just walking your dog?" asked Miranda.

"No," said Amos. "I was going to meet my friends. We'd planned a bonfire. A huge bonfire. We had lots of wood. We had hot chocolate and delicious marshmallows. We were ready for a long, happy party in the woods."

Scene 4

"So what happened?" asked Jean-Luc. "Were your friends there?"

"They were gathered around the fire," said Amos. "We were laughing and singing and talking. And eating, of course. Then, suddenly, a cold wind blew. Everyone stopped talking. The wind blew harder. It felt like an icy knife against our faces. The only sound was the wind. It sounded like a dog howling."

- Where was Amos going?
- Who was with him?
- What was the weather like?
- Why was Amos going into the woods?
- What were the friends doing?
- Why did everyone stop talking?

"It was just the wind," said Miranda, nervously.

"Yes, it was the wind, said Amos. "But it was an evil wind, a dark wind. It made us freeze. It made us afraid. The strange howling noise and the sudden chill of the wind made us tremble. Then there was a loud and terrible scream. Amber ran into the forest. Our wonderful fire went out. It just stopped burning. It was like an invisible giant foot stepped on it."

Scene 6

"We were in the cold, dark clearing," Amos continued. "Weak moonlight made strange shapes on the frozen ground. Then we heard it. It was a low, whispery voice, the voice of someone who hasn't spoken in a long, long time. It seemed to come from the ground. 'Leave me alone,' it said. 'Please, leave me alone.'"

Scene 7

Miranda and Jean-Luc gasped.

"We ran," said Amos. "We ran like cats in a rainstorm. We ran like scared rabbits. It was a terrible cold, dark night."

"Was someone playing a trick on you?" asked Jean-Luc.

Scene 8

"We didn't know," said Amos. "But I went back in the spring. The trees were green. The sun was shining. And in the clearing, near the ashes of our bonfire, I found a stone marker. It said, 'Here lies Margaret Grover. Fire took her from us. October 31, 1812.'"

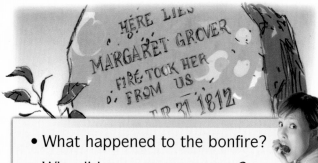

- What happened to the bonfire?
- Why did everyone run away?
- When did Amos go back?
- What did he find?

After You Read

- Look at all the words you wrote for each scene.
- Put them together in sentences to retell the story.

An old man is telling a story to two kids. It is about a forest called Grover's Grave.

THERE LIES
MARGARET GROVER.

ocabulary

clearing *n.* an open space in a forest
evil *adj.* very bad, wicked
scream *n.* shriek
trick *n.* something that deceives somebody
whispery *adj.* very quiet

BACKGROUND

Unexplained and mysterious events fascinate people of all ages. We all seem to enjoy a scary story, whether a campfire tale or a television series. Ghost stories have a long history and are told in almost every country. The ghosts may be malevolent or benevolent; they may bring good news or bad. They may appear only once or they may appear every year or every month. They may appear in only one special place or in several places.

Ghosts appear in movies, on television and in literature. Think of Casper, the friendly ghost, or the ghost in the legend of Sleepy Hollow. You can read about ghosts in stories by many great authors, including H. G. Wells, Sir Arthur Conan Doyle and Rudyard Kipling. Ghost stories are always popular.

Do you believe in ghosts?

ANOTHER KIND OF HERO

Before You Read

• Indicate if you think these statements are **true** or **false**.

   1. Heroes always perform extraordinary acts of bravery.

   2. For some people it is heroic to face daily life.

• Rate the activities described in
the following headlines.   1 = very courageous
                                  2 = courageous
                                  3 = somewhat courageous
                                  4 = not courageous

   1. Firefighter Saves Child from Building

   2. Teenager Fights Wild Dog in Local Park

   3. Students Fight Shopping Mall for Handicapped Access

   4. Local Soccer Team Loses Championship with a Smile

When You Read

• Make a note of new or interesting words.

• Think about the question(s) at the bottom
of the pages.

courageous: brave

trategy 14

Infer:
Make guesses based on what you already
know and on the clues in the text.

Dudley had a new joke everyday. He was always laughing and smiling and telling jokes. Jasmine liked that.

"Today's the big day," said Jasmine. "Excited? I am!"

"Not me. Prize Day never excites me." Dudley smiled. "They don't give out prizes for always forgetting your backpack. Hey, Jasmine, what do you call a headache in school?"

"I give up. What?"

"Aiken. Get it? Aching, like a pain and Aiken, like Ms. Aiken. They sound the same, right?" They both laughed. Ms. Aiken was the toughest teacher in the school and the hardest to please. She was Dudley's teacher.

Dudley walked to school everyday. Sometimes he forgot where the school was. Left at the lights or right at the corner? Sometimes he remembered. If Jasmine was waiting at the corner, they walked to school together. Jasmine was Dudley's friend.

If Fred Banks was waiting at the corner, Dudley took the long way to school. Fred Banks wasn't kind. He called Dudley names like Dopey Dudley and made fun of him because he spoke slowly.

Dudley saw Jasmine at the corner. He was safe.

"Hey, Dud!" Jasmine called.

"Hey, Jas!" Dudley answered. "Jas, what do you call a dentist with a drill in her hand?"

"I give up. What?"

"A toothache," Dudley said and they both laughed.

- What does Dudley sometimes forget?
- Why is Jasmine excited?

At school Dudley and Jasmine saw Fred and his friends. Fred made a loser sign on his forehead. His friends laughed. Dudley just smiled.

In class, Ms. Aiken told everyone to get ready for assembly. Fred tried to trip Dudley and shouted "Careful, dummy." Dudley smiled and said "I won't fall for that old trick, Fred," and stepped over Fred's foot. "Get it, Fred? Fall for it. That's a joke."

The assembly hall was full. All the students were waiting. The principal, Ms. Jain, started to announce the prizes. She gave the teacher, the reason for the award and then the name of the student.

Dudley sat between Jasmine and Kathleen. Fred sat behind them. He kicked Dudley's chair. Dudley didn't care. He was with his friends.

"Hey, Dudley!" Fred whispered. "I want you to applaud when I get Ms. Aiken's prize. Do you want me to show you how to applaud?"

Dudley just smiled and ignored him again.

They watched as students received their prizes: best in mathematics, best soccer player, highest marks in social studies. Everyone applauded after each name. Then Ms. Jain did somethng unusual. She asked Ms. Aiken to speak. Ms. Aiken stood straight and tall. Her bushy eyebrows made her look almost angry. She spoke loudly.

"Every year we give prizes for being the best," she said. "I have a different kind of prize to award. One boy comes to school every day and works very, very hard. He's my best student because he always tries. The work isn't easy for him but he smiles and keeps working. He always smiles, even when someone makes fun of him. He's brave because he never gives up. So, I'm giving him the award for Scholastic Courage. His name is Dudley White."

- What shows that Fred is unkind?

After You Read

- Think about one of your heroes. Why do you admire him or her?

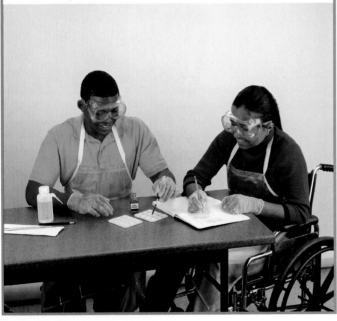

BACKGROUND

What does it take to be a hero? It takes courage and determination. Heroes are special people who do extraordinary things under difficult conditions. They are people to admire because they face challenges bravely. They struggle to overcome adversity.

Every four years athletes face the challenge of the Special Olympics. These athletes demonstrate the essence of heroism because they face and overcome difficulties to compete and succeed. They take and live the oath of the Special Olympics: "Let me win, but if I cannot win let me be brave in the attempt."

Shouldn't we all live by this simple promise?

As cool as a cucumber

Watch out! It's *raining cats and dogs*. Look at that boy. He has *ants in his pants*.

Do you think that there are really cats and dogs falling from the sky? Do you think that the boy really has ants in his pants? Of course not! These expressions shouldn't be taken literally. "It's raining cats and dogs" means that there is very heavy rain. "He has ants in his pants" means that the boy is excited and he can't sit still. These expressions can be very confusing for a person who is learning another language. If you think about what each word really means, then you will have a difficult time guessing what the expression means. You will have to *cross your fingers* or *knock on wood* and just hope for the best.

Expressions like this are called idioms. Idioms are expressions which cannot be understood by using only the meanings of the individual words. There are hundreds and hundreds of English idioms. Idioms make languages more interesting. Sometimes they can be very funny. Sometimes they provide us with an interesting image. Sometimes they help us express our emotions. They help us add variety to the way we speak and we all know that *variety is the spice of life!*

Here are some common English idioms with their meanings.

All thumbs: To be all thumbs means to be clumsy. Imagine what it would be like to have only thumbs and no fingers!

Beat a dead horse: To beat a dead horse means to insist on something even though it will not accomplish anything.

On top of the world

Butterflies in your stomach: To have butterflies in your stomach means to be very nervous about something. Imagine what it would be like to have butterflies flying around inside you!

Every Tom, Dick and Harry: In the Middle Ages, Thomas, Richard and Henry were common names. If you invite every Tom, Dick and Harry to a party, it means that you invite everybody you can—even people who are not particularly important to you.

Costs an arm and a leg: if something costs an arm and a leg, it is very expensive. Would you be willing to give up an arm and a leg to buy something?

Not my cup of tea.

Over your head: if something goes over your head it means that you are unable to understand it. Maybe these idioms are over your head!

Piece of cake: if something is very easy for you, it is a piece of cake. Are these idioms a piece of cake?

Put your foot down: To put your foot down means to make a firm decision and stick to it.

See eye to eye: To see eye to eye means to agree with someone about something. Often teenagers and their parents **don't** see eye to eye!

Sky's the limit: The sky's the limit means that there is no limit to what you can do or achieve.

What do you think the illustrated idioms mean? Trying to figure them out might *drive you crazy* but *go out on a limb* and *give it your best shot*!

PROJECTS

PROJECT

1

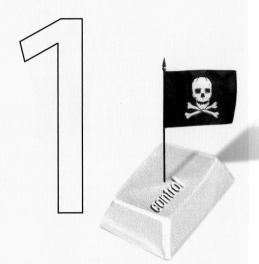

From High Seas to Cyberspace

The pirates of the past travelled the high seas looking for gold, spices and other goods. The pirates of the present steal music, software and even identities. The pirates and the treasures they look for may be very different but piracy still affects society. Discover new things about pirates and present your project to the class.

What do you want to find out about pirates of the past or present?

A. PLANNING

1. Write down what you already know about pirates of the past and pirates of the present.

2. Share your ideas with your classmates.

	What I know	What I learned
Pirates of the past	They looked for gold.	
Pirates of the present	They steal music.	

3. Decide what you want to learn more about.

4. Choose a focus for your project. For example:
   - similarities and differences between pirates of the past and present
   - pirate behaviour
   - pirate language
   - software piracy
   - music piracy
   - identity piracy

5. Form a team with classmates who are interested in the same subject as you.

6. List the things you already know about this subject.

7. Decide what you want to find out. Write questions to help you focus. For example:
   - What exactly is music piracy?
   - Who are the music pirates of today?
   - What are the effects of music piracy on society?
   - What can we do to help prevent music piracy?

8. Assign one question to each team member.

B. RESEARCH

1. Choose the resources you will consult. For example:
   - CD-ROMs
   - the Internet
   - magazines
   - movies
   - newspapers
   - an on-line encyclopaedia
   - people

2. If you use the Internet, think about key words you could use to research your subject.

3. Research your subject.

4. Take notes. Group your ideas into categories.

5. Share the information you find with your partners.

C. PREPARATION

1. With your partners, decide on a format for your project. Choose the one that is most appropriate.

For example:
- a CD cover about music piracy
- a comic strip
- a dramatic sketch
- a pirate's code of conduct
- a poster about software piracy
- a print or on-line dictionary of pirate expressions
- a Venn diagram or other graphic organizer to compare different types of pirates
- a 'wanted' poster about identity pirates

2. Make a list of what you will need for your project.

3. Assign roles and responsibilities to each team member.

4. Bring the material you need to class.

5. Practise your presentation with another team.

D. PRESENTATION

Present your project to your classmates.

We found information on the Internet.

We decided to present the information on posters.

We chose software piracy.

We each made a poster. I did the first one.

PROJECT 2

A PASSION FOR FASHION

Fashion is what you wear and how you wear it. It includes not just clothes, but hair styles, shoes and accessories. Fashion makes a statement. It says something about who you are. Some styles say "I'm a skateboarder" or "I'm a basketball fan." Others say "I'm current." Some teens model their styles on their favourite stars or sports heroes. Some teens create an individual style.

What is today's style?
What is your style?

A. PLANNING

1. Choose an aspect of fashion to present. For example:
   - a current style that teens are wearing
   - a new style you want to design
   - traditional dress from a particular country
   - your design for a school uniform

2. Form a team with classmates interested in the same topic.

B. RESEARCH

1. Make a list of the resources you will consult. For example:

   - books
   - catalogues
   - the Internet
   - magazines
   - newspapers

2. Find as much information about your choice as you can.

3. Look at fashion pages for ideas on different ways to present fashion.

C. PREPARATION

1. With your partners, decide how you will present your project. For example, as:

   - an advertisement
   - a fashion show
   - a poster
   - a Web page

2. Make a list of everything you need.

3. Assign roles and responsibilities to each team member.

D. PRESENTATION

Present your fashion project to your classmates.

What Today's Skateboarder Wears

Baseball cap. Sometimes the cap is worn sideways or back to front.

Big hoodie

Logos of skateboarding companies or sports teams are common.

Cargo pants with lots of pockets. Pants are loose so you can move easily.

Skateboarding shoes

6

Teens on Air

Teens spend a lot of time watching television and listening to the radio. Many programs deal with news, reviews, fashion, music, sports and other topics of interest to a teenage audience. Some programs are even hosted by teens.

This project gives you a chance to research, write and present a program unique to you and your friends.

What kind of program would you like to present? What topics would interest teens in your community?

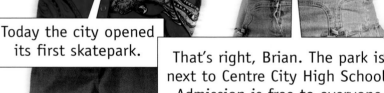

Today the city opened its first skatepark.

That's right, Brian. The park is next to Centre City High School. Admission is free to everyone from 13 to 19.

The latest DVD from this group is not very good. The colours are too dull and there is no connection between the images and the songs. Don't buy "Midnight Movies."

A. PLANNING

1. With your partners, choose the topic or topics you will present.
2. Choose one or more segments of your television program. For example:
   - an interview
   - a media review (movie, CD or television program)
   - a newscast
   - a panel discussion about a current event of interest to you and your partners

B. RESEARCH

1. Make a list of the resources you will consult for information on your topic. For example:
   - books
   - catalogues
   - the Internet
   - magazines
   - newspapers

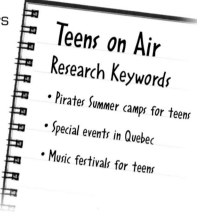

Teens on Air
Research Keywords
- Pirates Summer camps for teens
- Special events in Quebec
- Music festivals for teens

2. Select a program to watch or listen to for ideas on presentation and language.
3. Assign each team member a specific research task.
4. Consult your teacher for ideas and suggestions.
5. Share your research with your partners.

C. PREPARATION

1. Assign roles and responsibilities to each team member.
2. Write a draft of what each person will say. Check and correct each draft.
3. Make a list of all the materials you will need. For example, visual supports such as maps and charts.
4. Review strategies you might need during your presentation.
5. Practise.

Teens on Air
Program Format
- Speaker announces events
- Reviewer rates events for teens
- Two teens talk about one of the events

D. PRESENTATION

Present your program to your classmates.

- Baker
- Butcher
- Cook
- Eastwood
- Hill
- Johnson
- O'Henry
- Peterson
- Redhead
- Short
- Rivers
- Smith
- White
- Williams
- Young

Before the twelfth century, people in England did not have surnames. They did not need them. Because villages were quite small and people usually knew one another, it was enough to refer to people by their first name.

But by the 1300s, approximately fifty percent of boys in any English village had one of the following names: Henry, John, Richard, Robert, Thomas or William. Imagine a village where four boys were called just William! There was certainly a need to find a way to distinguish who was who and which William was which, so people would talk about William the son of Peter, William who lives by the woods, William the baker and William who has red hair. These descriptions eventually became shorter, and the four boys named William were called William Peterson, William Woods, William Baker and William Redhead. This made things much easier.

Today most English surnames still fall into the same categories: names derived from first names, names derived from the place where the person lived, names that refer to the person's occupation and names that refer to or a physical attribute such as body shape, facial traits and hair colour.

Many people of Irish descent have names such as McDonald, O'Brien or Fitzpatrick. Many Scottish people also have Mac names. *Mac* or *Mc* means son and *O* means grandson so MacDonald would mean the son of Donald and O'Connor would be the grandson of Connor. *Fitz* is an Irish word which comes from the Norman word *fis* (son). Fitzpatrick means son of Patrick.

To find out the origins of the surnames on the left, ask the following questions about each one.

Who is the person's father?

Where did the person come from?

What is the person's job?

What is the person's special feature or trait?

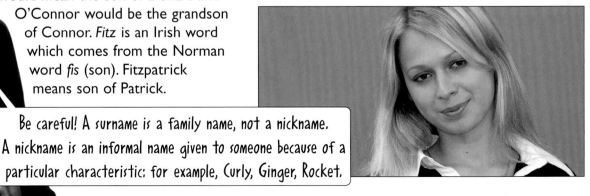

> Be careful! A surname is a family name, not a nickname. A nickname is an informal name given to someone because of a particular characteristic: for example, Curly, Ginger, Rocket.

PORTFOLIO PAUSES

141

PORTFOLIO PAUSE 1
Leaving a Trace

I loved reading the stories and I'm very proud of my Reader's Journal.

Revision

- Think about three pieces of work you did in English class last year.
- For each one, provide the information below.
- Tell a partner about each piece.
- Complete the personal profile for your portfolio.

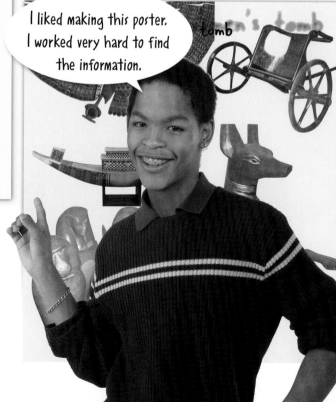

I liked making this poster. I worked very hard to find the information.

1. Title of work
2. What the work shows:
   - how I interact orally with others in English
   - how I understand a text
   - how I write
3. Why I remember this work

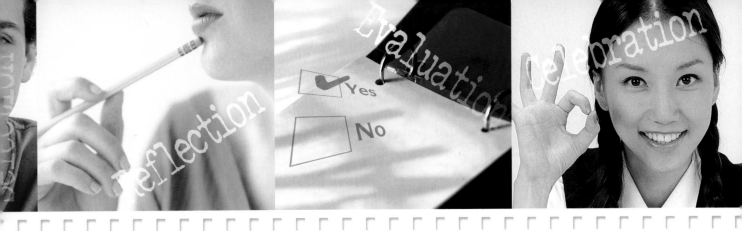

Preparation

- Review the portfolio process.
- Personalize the front cover of your portfolio.
- Prepare the cover page.

The Portfolio Process

1. Collect your work.
2. Think about what you have to include in your portfolio. Select pieces to meet the requirements. (Look for this message at the end of each unit, story or project. It will remind you to choose material.)
3. Reflect on each piece of work. Explain what it represents and why it is important.
4. Present your portfolio for evaluation.
5. Celebrate your work and your progress.

Selection

- Listen to your teacher.
- Write the requirements on your cover page.
- Select items for your portfolio.

Reflection

- Complete a reflection coupon for each piece of work.
- Begin the table of contents for your portfolio.

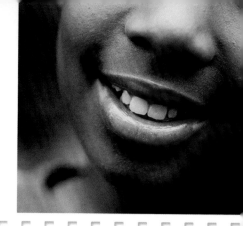

PORTFOLIO PAUSE 2
Making a Choice

Selection

- Listen to your teacher.
- List the requirements for Term 2 on the cover page of your portfolio.
- Group your work into the following categories.
    1. Work that shows how you interact with others in English
    2. Work that shows how well you understand a text
    3. Work that shows how you write or produce texts
- Select items for your portfolio.
- Share your ideas with a partner.
- Help each other find appropriate items for your portfolios.

Reflection

- Think about the items you selected.
- Provide a short reflection piece for each item. Use the following questions for help.
    1. What does this piece show?
    2. Why did I choose this piece?
    3. What did I learn while doing this work?
    4. Which strategies did I use while doing this work?
    5. What would I change if I did the work again?
- Add information to your table of contents.

If I did the work again, I'd check it more carefully.

I put my quiz in my portfolio because I really enjoyed this activity.

It's a great quiz. I like the topic, Discover Your Party Profile. That was a neat idea.

Thanks. Which piece did you choose to show how you write?

I chose the text I wrote about school today. I worked really hard on it. I wrote a rough copy and then I checked my work. I followed the steps in the writing process. I think I did a good job.

Presentation

- Present your portfolio to a partner.
- Listen to your partner's presentation.
- Tell your partner what you think about his or her work.

Evaluation

- Listen to your teacher.
- Prepare the evaluation section of your portfolio.

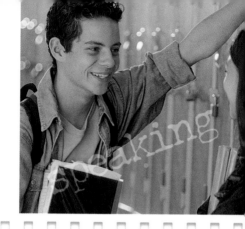

PORTFOLIO PAUSE 3
Getting Ready

Selection and Reflection

- Select items for your portfolio.
- Provide a reflection piece for each item.
- Use the information in **Portfolio Pause 2** and the questions on the right for help.

Questions to ask yourself when you select work for your portfolio

SPEAKING

1. What type of activity is represented here: a discussion, conversation, presentation, other?
2. Which strategies did I use when I did this activity?
3. Do I think my speaking has improved? Why or why not?
4. What new words and expressions did I learn when I did this activity?
5. Did I use resources when I did this activity? Which ones?

READING OR LISTENING TO A TEXT

1. Did I read, view or listen to the text before I did this piece?
2. Which strategies did I use to help me understand the text?
3. Does this piece show how I reuse information from a text?
4. What did I learn when I did this activity?
5. What was the most difficult thing about this piece of work?

WRITING OR PRODUCING A TEXT

1. How did this piece change from the rough draft to the good copy?
2. Is there evidence that I checked and corrected my work?
3. Which strategies did I use when I wrote or produced this piece?
4. What would I like to improve in this piece?
5. What is the best thing about this piece of work?

Preparation

- Get ready to present your portfolio.
- Use this information for help.

Things to check when you prepare your portfolio

PRESENTATION AND ORGANIZATION

1. My portfolio is well-organized.
2. The items are in chronological order.
3. My table of contents is up-to-date.
4. My portfolio is personalized and shows my creativity.

CONTENTS

I have included:
- items that show how I speak English, how I understand texts and how I write and produce texts
- a variety of items such as audio recordings, CDs, checklists, drawings, photographs, questionnaires, video recordings and written work
- items that show how I work alone, with a partner and with a team
- a reflection piece for each item

This piece shows how I work with a partner.

Quiz Me!

cont. →

cont.

- Practise with your partners.
- Use the questions on the right for help.

Questions to ask yourself when you present your portfolio

ABOUT THE WORK

1. Which piece is my favourite? Why?
2. Which piece am I most proud of? Why?
3. Which piece best shows my creativity?
4. Which piece shows how I work with others?
5. Which piece was the most difficult?
6. What do I like best about this piece?
7. What are the strengths of this piece?
8. How much time did I spend on this piece?
9. Which strategies did I use when doing this work?
10. Which processes did I use to complete this work?

ABOUT THE PORTFOLIO

1. Would I rate my portfolio as excellent, very good, satisfactory or unsatisfactory? Why?
2. What does my portfolio show about me?
3. How did I decide which pieces to include?
4. Did I like working on my portfolio?
5. How do I feel when I look at the work I have done?

I rate my portfolio as excellent because . . .

I will work towards this goal by. . . .

Reflection

- Think about what you still need to improve.
- Set an end-of-cycle goal for yourself.

Presentation

- Present your portfolio.

PORTFOLIO PAUSE 4
Putting It All Together

Selection and Reflection

- Select items for your portfolio.

- Provide a reflection piece for each item.

- Group your work into the following categories.

  1. Work that shows how you interact with others in English

  2. Work that shows how well you understand a text

  3. Work that shows how you write or produce texts.

- Think about the end-of-cycle goal you set for yourself. Ask yourself the following questions.

- Check your portfolio to make sure that everything is in order.

- Use the information in the Preparation section of **PORTFOLIO PAUSE 3** for help.

- Read the model letter on page 154.

Questions to ask yourself about your end-of-cycle goal

1. What was my end-of-cycle goal?

2. Did I achieve this goal? Why or why not?

3. What would I do differently next time?

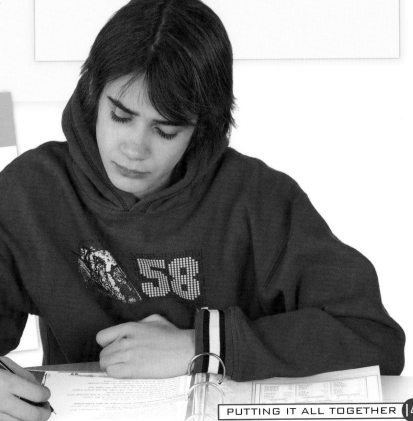

May 30

Dear Mr. Rousseau,

This portfolio shows work from my Secondary Cycle One English class. It shows what I've learned and how my English has improved. It also contains activities that show how I work with my classmates. You'll find a table of contents with the items listed in chronological order. I hope you find that my portfolio is well-organized and interesting to read.

To show how I speak English, I decided to include the video of my performance piece from last year. I wrote a rap about protecting the environment. When I wrote the rap, I thought about the environment and the consequences that our actions have on it. I also learned about performing in front of a group. I learned to relax, to articulate my words, to project my voice and to make eye contact with my audience. Most of all, I learned to have fun! This work also shows how I work with others. I had fun working with my partner, Richard Warren. We worked very well together.

My second piece is the recording of our group discussion from Unit 2, "Places and Traces." We talked about school and shared our opinions with one another. I particularly liked this activity because we had time to discuss things with our teacher. I planned my work with my partners and then we listened to one another, took notes and used this information in our texts. This activity helped me with question formation. You'll see that I didn't make any mistakes in my questions.

In Unit 7, "When Disaster Strikes," we read newspaper articles about different disasters. I loved this activity because I learned a lot about the past. I decided to include this activity to show how I understand texts. I learned to use different strategies while reading—for example, to look at the headlines and find the important words.

I also included my dictionary of sports expressions from Unit 8, "Sport in the Classroom." I love sports so I really like the idea of using language about my favourite thing. I use a lot of these expressions when I talk now.

To show how I write and produce texts, I chose two texts. The first text is a poster about Internet piracy. I researched the topic and then I used the information I found to make a 'wanted' poster for Internet pirates. This activity helped me to use different technologies. You can see I had problems with my spelling. I didn't check my work very carefully.

The second piece is the ending to the story A Cold, Dark Night. I wrote this with a partner. This time, I did my best to check my work. I didn't make very many mistakes. I think my ideas were creative. I really used my imagination and I am proud of this story.

I hope you'll see that I put a lot of effort into my work. I'm very proud of it and satisfied with my progress. I think I did a good job in class this year. Thank you for your help.

Sincerely,

Elizabeth Raymond

Presentation and Evaluation

- Write a letter to present your portfolio. Use the contents of your portfolio, your reflection pieces, the model letter and the notes on the writing process on pages 166 and 167 for help.
- Place the letter in your portfolio.
- Make sure your table of contents is up-to-date.
- Submit your portfolio for evaluation.

Celebration

- Choose five of your best pieces. Try to show a variety of work.
- Label each piece.
- Present the work to your partners.
- Comment on your partners' presentations.

> That's great work, Elizabeth. I learned a lot about Internet piracy from your presentation.

> This is my presentation about Internet piracy. It shows how I used information and different technologies.

COMMUNICATION STRATEGIES

> I love pizza. It's so tasty.

> My number is 876-8876.

> 876-8876?

1. GESTURE
Use actions to help transmit your message.

2. RECAST
Check if you understand someone by repeating what she or he says.

> This CD is great. It's awesome. Fabulous. Super.

> Just a moment, please.

> It's the thing I use for my bike. To fix the tire.

3. REPHRASE
Use different words to say the same thing.

4. STALL FOR TIME
Show that you need more time to think of your response.

5. SUBSTITUTE
When you don't know the word for something, try to describe it.

LEARNING STRATEGIES

6. DIRECT ATTENTION
Focus your attention. Don't be distracted.

7. PAY SELECTIVE ATTENTION
Decide what you should pay attention to before you start your work.

8. PLAN
Think about what you need to do to achieve a goal.

9. SELF-EVALUATE
Reflect on what you have learned.

10. SELF-MONITOR
Check and correct your work.

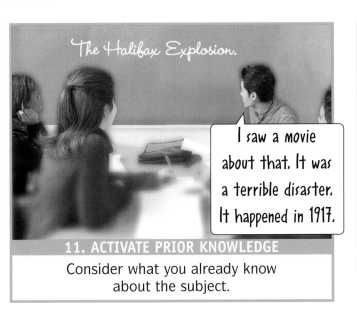

11. ACTIVATE PRIOR KNOWLEDGE
Consider what you already know about the subject.

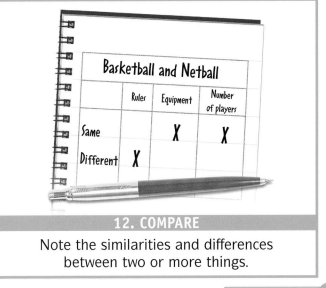

12. COMPARE
Note the similarities and differences between two or more things.

What is the first clue?

Er. The first clue. Yes. The tea cup.

13. DELAY SPEAKING

Listen carefully. Take your time and respond when you feel comfortable.

EMERGENCY
RESPONSE PLAN

I know what that means. It's almost the same in French.

14. INFER

Make guesses based on what you already know and on the clues in the text.

'ello. 'ow are you? Hello. 'ow are you? Hello. How are you?

15. PRACTISE

Reuse language until you get it right.

I think this unit is about a special place for teenagers.

16. PREDICT

Make a hypothesis based on the information you already have.

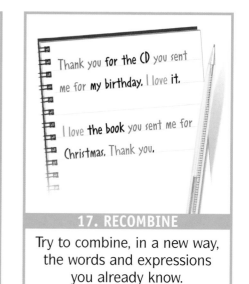

Thank you for the CD you sent me for my birthday. I love it.

I love the book you sent me for Christmas. Thank you.

17. RECOMBINE

Try to combine, in a new way, the words and expressions you already know.

TRISTAN AND ISOLDE
WALK THE LINE

18. SCAN

Look or listen for specific information.

modern pirates, computers

19. SKIM

Read through a text quickly to get a general overview.

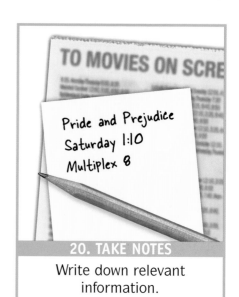

TO MOVIES ON SCRE

Pride and Prejudice
Saturday 1:10
Multiplex 8

20. TAKE NOTES

Write down relevant information.

21. USE SEMANTIC MAPPING

Group similar ideas together.

22. ASK FOR HELP, REPETITION, CLARIFICATION, CONFIRMATION

Request assistance.

23. COOPERATE

Work with others to achieve a goal.

24. ENCOURAGE YOURSELF AND OTHERS

Reward yourself and congratulate your classmates.

25. LOWER ANXIETY

Relax. Laugh. Remember your successes and focus on your progress.

26. TAKE RISKS

Experiment and don't be afraid to make mistakes.

CUE CARDS

Getting to know someone

1

► **Colour** = use your own words.

► Hello, my name is **Nat**.
► Pleased to meet you.
► What's your name?
► How's it going?
► What's new?

Identifying someone

2

► This is **my partner**.
► She's in my class.

Talking on the phone/leaving a message

Hello. Is Joshua there, please?

He isn't here at the moment. Can I take a message?

Please can you ask him to call Sara. My number's 576-9804.

O.K. Bye.

Goodbye.

▶ May I speak to **Sylvie**, please?

▶ This message is for **Denise**.

▶ This is **Dan**.

▶ My name is **Pat**.

▶ I'm calling about **the dance**.

▶ I'll call back.

▶ Please call back.

Filling time while you think

▶ So . . .

▶ You see . . .

▶ Well . . .

▶ Give me a second.

What's the quickest way to the library?

Um. Let me think. O.K. Walk up Viger and then go across the park.

CUE CARDS

Apologizing

5

- ▶ I apologize for **being rude**.
- ▶ Excuse me.

Checking up

6

- ▶ What do you think?
- ▶ What about you?
- ▶ Is this clear?

Warning

7

- ▶ Pay attention!
- ▶ Watch out!

Politely interrupting a conversation

C 8

► Sorry to interrupt.

Agreeing, disagreeing and giving an opinion

C 9

► I disagree.

► I don't think so.
We disagree.
They believe it was
Jacques Cartier.

Talking about capabilities

C 10

► I'm sure we can.
► We're able to **make a model**.

11 Talking about feelings, interests, tastes and preferences

I don't like hockey, I prefer basketball.

▶ I'm sad.
▶ I hate **winter**.
▶ He likes **reading**.
▶ They enjoy **Chinese food**.

12 Expressing decision and indecision

I choose chocolate.

I don't know which flavour I want.

▶ I decided to **visit Ben**.
▶ She's not sure about that.
▶ They've decided to **play chess**.

13 Asking for permission

▶ Can you **buy me a ticket**?

Dad, please may I see Rufus Wainwright?

Asking for and giving advice

► Is this the right thing to do?

► I think that **you should work harder**.

Giving instructions and talking about classroom routines

► Write this down.

► Whose turn is it?

Offering and requesting help

► Can I help you?

► Do you need help?

► Do you need a hand?

► Can I give you a hand?

CUE CARDS

Asking for help

- How do you say *casquette* in English?
- Could you help me?
- How do we do this?
- Is this right?

Asking for information

- Do you have **a pencil**?
- **Who** is the team recorder?
- **What** is the time?
- **When** is the hockey game?
- **Where** can I find a ruler?
- **Why** is Jeanine crying?
- **How** old are you?
- **How much** does it cost?
- **How many** students are on the bus?

Suggesting and inviting

- Let's do a **project on music**.
- How about **hip-hop**?
- Would you like to join our team?

20

Working in a team and encouraging each other

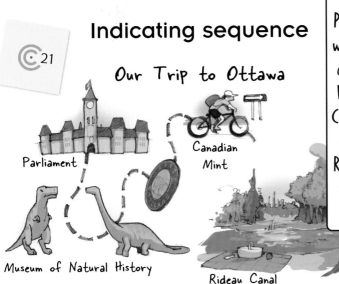

- ► Good work!
- ► Let's put our heads together.
- ► You're **the team secretary**.
- ► We're doing well.

20 21

Indicating sequence

Our Trip to Ottawa

Parliament

Canadian Mint

Museum of Natural History

Rideau Canal

First, we visited Parliament. Then we went to the Museum of Natural History. We also visited the Canadian Mint. Next, we rode along the Rideau Canal. Finally, we had a picnic at Dows Lake.

- ► So **we went home**.
- ► We also **saw the Peace Tower**.

22

Saying goodbye

Take care.

See you soon.

Bye!

- ► That's all I have to say.
- ► I have to go.
- ► Bye for now.

Did you know that advertisements, conversations, signs, television shows, videos and Web sites are all texts? A text is not just something you read. A text is any form of communication. You can read, listen to or view a text.

Here are some tips to help you understand a text. Don't forget to use a dictionary, the strategies (pages 152–155) and the word list (pages 172–174).

STEP 1 GET READY

You can

- look at the headline or title and predict what the text is about (Strategy 16)

- look at the photos or illustrations and make guesses about the text (Strategy 14)

I know what that means. It's almost the same in French.

14. INFER

Make guesses based on what you already know and on the clues in the text.

- think about what you already know (Strategy 11)

STEP 2 AS YOU RESPOND

1. Focus on the text

- Think about how you are working. Think about what you are learning.

- Look or listen for specific information. (Strategy 18)

- Find the general meaning of the text. (Strategy 19)

- Organize ideas into groups. (Strategy 21)

- Relax. Don't worry if you don't understand everything. (Strategy 25)

18. SCAN

Look or listen for specific information.

- You can also take notes: write down your ideas, key words and questions you have about the text. (Strategy 20)

2. Share your reactions

- Share your reaction to the text with your classmates and teacher. (Strategy 23)

- Listen to your classmates' ideas. Find out what they think about the text. If you don't understand something, ask your classmates or your teacher for help. (Strategy 22)

I found that . . .

I learned . . .

I understood . . .

I'm not sure about . . .

3. Make connections

- Connect the ideas in the text to your personal experiences. Share your ideas with your classmates.
- Think about how the ideas in the text apply to your community and society.

I feel like X because . . .

I had an experience like . . . ,

The part about X made me think about . . .

The music makes me feel . . .

I wish everyone would . . . ,

I think we should all . . .

People need to . . .

STEP 3 AFTERWARDS

- Do an activity to show what you learned.
- Reflect. Think about one thing you are proud of. Think about one thing you can improve next time. (Strategy 9)
- Congratulate yourself and your classmates on your good work. (Strategy 24)

4. Share your ideas

- Discuss your ideas with your classmates and your teacher.

Great job!

24. ENCOURAGE YOURSELF AND OTHERS
Reward yourself and congratulate your classmates.

PROCESSES

The writing process has four steps: preparing to write, writing, revising and editing.

Depending on the text, you may move back and forth between the steps. When you write short, informal texts, you may not need to go through all the steps.

STEP 1 GET READY

1. Think about the following questions.

- WHO is going to read your text?
  You can write for
    - a particular person (for example, a teacher, a parent, a friend, a young child)
    - a particular group of people (for example, a class of students, a group of children, a group which represents a particular culture)

- WHY are you writing your text?

- WHAT TYPE OF TEXT do you want to write?

- WHAT DO YOU WANT TO SHARE with your audience?

2. Brainstorm about your subject.

- Think about what you already know. Write down lots of words. Jot down some ideas and personal memories. (Strategy 11)

3. Find out more about your subject.

- Make a list of resources to consult.

- Research your topic.

4. Plan your work.

- Write an outline of your text. (Strategy 8)

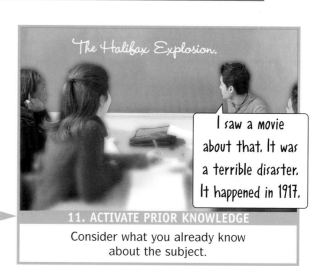

> I saw a movie about that. It was a terrible disaster. It happened in 1917.

11. ACTIVATE PRIOR KNOWLEDGE

Consider what you already know about the subject.

To Do
1. Go on the Internet
2. Search for pirates
3. ~~crackers~~
4. Fam~~

8. PLAN

Think about what you need to do to achieve a goal.

STEP 2 WRITE THE TEXT

1. Focus on the way you work.

- Think about how you are working. Are you satisfied with your text? Are you satisfied with your effort?

2. Write a draft.

- Look at your plan for help.

- Write everything you can about your subject.

- Don't reject any ideas yet. Don't worry about making mistakes. (Strategy 26)

> I bought a new dictionary at the library. You know, librairie? Oh no, not the library. The **bookstore**.

26. TAKE RISKS

Experiment and don't be afraid to make mistakes.

5. Share your ideas.

- Discuss your ideas with your teacher and your classmates. Ask them to comment on your ideas and your plan. (Strategy 23)

STEP 3   REVISE YOUR TEXT

1. Read what you wrote.

- Decide what needs to be improved.

2. Consult other people.

- Ask your teacher or a classmate to read your text. Find out what they think about it. Ask them for suggestions. (Strategy 22)

- Read or listen to your teacher's or classmate's comments.

3. Reflect on your work.

- Reflect on what your classmate or teacher said. (Strategy 9)

- Read your text again.

- Answer the following questions.
  - Is my text well organized?
  - Are my paragraphs well organized?
  - Did I choose the right words?
  - Do I need to add, delete or change anything?

- Read your text aloud to hear how it sounds.

The answer is elephant.

How do you spell that?

e–l–e–p–h–a–n–t

22. ASK FOR HELP, REPETITION, CLARIFICATION, CONFIRMATION

Request assistance.

STEP 4   EDIT YOUR TEXT

1. Check for errors.

- Use a dictionary and the resources in Centre Stage: the grammar boxes and the language models throughout the book and the word list on pages 172–174.

- Check and correct
  - sentence structure
  - language use
  - capitalization
  - punctuation
  - spelling
  (Strategy 10)

Julia and Chloe finds a clue.

10. SELF-MONITOR

Check and correct your work.

2. Ask a classmate to check your text.

3. Read your text again to see if anything else needs to be changed.

PUBLISH YOUR TEXT

When you have written your text, decide if you are going to share it with an audience. If so, follow these steps.

1. Choose an appropriate format.

- Think about how you will present your text visually.

2. Prepare a final copy.

- Write the final copy neatly in ink or use the computer.

3. Check your work.

- Read your text again.

- Ask a classmate to read your text again.

- Make the necessary corrections.

- Take the **POP** quiz. If you answer yes to all three questions, you are ready to publish your text.

P for Proofreading: Did I check my text one last time? Did I use correct punctuation and capitalization? Did I check my spelling?

O for Organization: Are my ideas organized logically? Is my message clear? Will my audience understand what I wrote?

P for Presentation: Is my text neatly written? Does it look attractive? Does it show that I have made an effort to work hard? Is my text ready to publish?

REFLECT ON YOUR WORK

Think about one thing you are proud of. Think about one thing you can improve next time. (Strategy 9)

PROCESSES

Advertisements, banners, billboards, computer games, magazines, multimedia computer presentations, music videos, newspapers, photo stories, posters, radio shows, videos and Web pages are all examples of media texts. There are three steps in the production process. Depending on the text, you may not need to follow all the steps.

STEP 1 PREPRODUCTION

1. **Think about the following questions.**
   - WHO will read, watch or listen to your text?
   - WHAT do you want to share with your audience?

2. **Brainstorm to find your subject.**

3. **Choose the type of media text that you will produce.**

4. **Think of a focus sentence that explains what you will do.**
   - Write this sentence down and refer to it often. It will help keep you on track. For example:

5. **Consider what you already know about your subject.** (Strategy 11)

6. **Plan ahead and prepare your work.**
   - Make a list of resources you can consult. (Strategy 8)

7. **Find out more about your subject.**

8. **Create a storyboard.**
   - Think about the type of communication you will use.
   - List the language or special elements necessary for that type of text: for example, persuasive language, background music, sound effects, camera close-ups. (Strategy 21)

> My team will make a video to promote tolerance of skateboarding.

Outdoor	Indoor
hockey	air hockey
baseball	video games
	pool

21. USE SEMANTIC MAPPING
Group similar ideas together.

> I'll design a poster to warn people about Internet piracy.

9. **Talk about your ideas with your classmates or your teacher.** (Strategy 23)

23. COOPERATE

Work with others to achieve a goal.

STEP 2 PRODUCTION

1. **Focus on the way you work.**

   - Think about how you are working. Are you satisfied with your product? Do you think your message will have the effect you want?

2. **Think about the specific techniques you will need to use and the elements to include.**

   - Choose
     - catchy headlines
     - slogans
     - symbols
     - narration
     - visual effects
     - images
     - sound effects

3. **Follow the writing process on pages 166 and 167.**

STEP 3 POSTPRODUCTION

1. **Edit and put the final touches on your product.**

2. **Present your media text to your audience.**

REFLECT ON YOUR WORK

Think about one thing you are proud of. Think about one thing you can improve next time. (Strategy 9)

I learned how to check my written work.

9. SELF-EVALUATE

Reflect on what you have learned.

FOCUS ON FORM

GRAMMAR EXPLANATIONS IN *Centre Stage 2*

COMMON IRREGULAR VERBS

INFINITIVE (TO . . .)	SIMPLE PAST	PAST PARTICIPLE
be	was/were	been
become	became	become
begin	began	begun
bite	bit	bitten
blow	blew	blown
break	broke	broken
bring	brought	brought
build	built	built
burn	burned	burnt
buy	bought	bought
catch	caught	caught
choose	chose	chosen
come	came	come
cost	cost	cost
cut	cut	cut
dig	dug	dug
do	did	done
draw	drew	drawn
drink	drank	drunk
drive	drove	driven
eat	ate	eaten
fall	fell	fallen
feel	felt	felt
fight	fought	fought
find	found	found
fly	flew	flown
forget	forgot	forgotten
forgive	forgave	forgiven
freeze	froze	frozen
get	got	got(ten)
give	gave	given
go	went	gone
grow	grew	grown
have	had	had
hear	heard	heard
hit	hit	hit
hold	held	held
hurt	hurt	hurt
keep	kept	kept
know	knew	known
lay (an egg)	laid	laid
lead	led	led

INFINITIVE (TO . . .)	SIMPLE PAST	PAST PARTICIPLE
leave	left	left
lend	lent	lent
let	let	let
lie (down)	lay	laid
lose	lost	lost
make	made	made
mean	meant	meant
meet	met	met
pay	paid	paid
put	put	put
read	read	read
ride	rode	ridden
run	ran	run
say	said	said
see	saw	seen
sell	sold	sold
send	sent	sent
shake	shook	shaken
shine	shone	shone
sing	sang	sung
sink	sank	sunk
sit	sat	sat
sleep	slept	slept
speak	spoke	spoken
spend	spent	spent
stand	stood	stood
steal	stole	stolen
sting	stung	stung
stink	stank	stunk
swear	swore	sworn
swim	swam	swum
take	took	taken
teach	taught	taught
tell	told	told
think	thought	thought
throw	threw	thrown
understand	understood	understood
wake	woke	woken
wear	wore	worn
win	won	won
write	wrote	written

ARTICLES

► The definite article (*the*) refers to a specific person, place or thing.
I saw the boy who lives next door.

► The indefinite articles (*a, an*) refer to any person, place or thing.
Beat an egg in a bowl.
Note. Use *an* before a vowel sound and *a* before a consonant sound.

CONJUNCTIONS

Conjunctions join two or more words or sentences.

► *And* joins two words or ideas.
Both my mother and my father came to the meeting.

► *Or* indicates an alternative.
Do you like strawberry or vanilla ice cream?

► *But* indicates the opposite.
I wanted to go to the party but I couldn't because I was ill.

► *So* indicates a result.
I missed the bus so I was late for school.

DETERMINERS AND PRONOUNS

Determiners and pronouns are used in place of proper nouns.

	Singular	Plural
Subject	I you he/she/it	we you they
Object	me you him/her/it	us you them
Possessive (before the noun)	my your his/her/its	our your their
Possessive (after the noun)	mine yours his/hers	ours yours theirs
Reflexive/emphatic	myself yourself himself/herself/itself	ourselves yourselves themselves

CAPITALIZATION

Use a *capital* letter for

► the pronoun *I*
I don't like winter but I love summer.

► the first word of every sentence
This book is very interesting.
My best friend is Elizabeth.
She is fourteen years old.

► proper nouns: the names of people, nationalities, languages and places
Thomas is Australian. He speaks English and lives in Sydney.

► titles and relationship words if used as part of a name
Doctor Martin, Professor Therrien and Aunt Jemima went to the dance.
Note. Don't capitalize the relationship word if it comes after a possessive pronoun (my, your, his, her, its, our, their): *my doctor, your uncle, her professor.*

► the names of specific school courses:
English 214, French 306
Note. Don't capitalize subjects: geography, history, mathematics, science.

► the months of the year, days of the week and holidays
January, February, March
Monday, Tuesday, Wednesday
Christmas, Hanukkah, Valentine's Day
Note. Don't capitalize the seasons: *spring, summer, fall, winter.*

► the first word of a direct quotation
The teacher said, "Always be on time."

► the first, last and important words in the title of a book, film, television show or song
Centre Stage
Me, Myself and I
Over the Rainbow
Note. Don't capitalize articles, prepositions or conjunctions.

WORD LIST

A

allowance *n.* pocket money (U1)

angle *n.* the space between two straight lines that meet (U8)

anniversary *n.* a date that is special because it is exactly a year or a number of years after an important event (U4)

to argue *v.* to disagree with someone in words, often in an angry way (U5)

available *adj.* able or ready to be used (U6)

awesome *adj.* very good (U3)

B

backup *n.* a copy of a computer document, program etc, which is made in case the original becomes lost or damaged (S1)

bad language *n.* swearing (U5)

bagpipe *n.* a traditional Scottish instrument (U4)

to battle *v.* to fight (U10)

to be inclined *v.* to have a tendency (U9)

beach *n.* an area of sand next to the sea (U2)

beam *n.* a long straight heavy piece of wood or metal (U7)

beginning *n.* start (U4)

bin *n.* a large container (U6)

birthday *n.* the date in each year on which you were born (U4)

boring *adj.* not interesting in any way (U3)

to be born *v.* to start to exist (U2)

to borrow *v.* to use something that belongs to someone else and that you must give back to them later (U3)

brain *n.* the organ inside your head that controls how you think, feel and move (U9)

to break *v.* to damage (U6)

C

candle *n.* a long piece of wax with a piece of string through the middle, which you burn to use as a light (U4)

cartoon instructions *n.* instructions in picture form (U2)

challenge *n.* something that tests strength or ability (S2)

chat room *n.* a place on the Internet where you can send and receive instant messages (U5)

clearing *n.* an open space in a forest (S3)

clue *n.* an object or piece of information that helps someone solve a crime or mystery (S2)

commercial break *n.* a pause in TV or radio programming for advertisements (U5)

computer *n.* an electronic machine that stores information and uses programs to help you find, organize, or change the information (U3)

to congratulate *v.* to tell someone that you are happy because they have achieved something (U3)

container *n.* something such as a bag or a box that you keep things in (U2)

cooking pot *n.* a metal container for heating food (U6)

country *n.* land that is not near towns or cities (U2)

crew *n.* the group of people who work on a ship (U7)

to criticize *v.* to say that someone or something is bad in some way (U5)

crypt *n.* an underground room, used in the past for burying people (U2)

cyber *prefix* relating to computers, especially to messages and information on the internet (S1)

D

date *n.* a small sweet brown fruit (U4)

deliberate *adj.* planned, not by accident (U7)

disease *n.* illness (U8)

disgusting *adj.* repugnant (U1)

to dislike *v.* to not like (U5)

disposable *adj.* designed to be used for a short time and then thrown away (U6)

Don't hold your breath. *idiom* Don't wait anxiously. (U2)

driveway *n.* the paved area or road between the street and a house (U5)

during *prep.* from the beginning to the end of a period of time (U3)

E

earthquake *n.* a sudden shaking of the earth's surface (U7)

emergency *n.* an unexpected and dangerous situation that must be dealt with immediately (U7)

to enjoy *v.* to get pleasure from something (U3)

escape route *n.* a way of getting away from a dangerous situation (U7)

everything *pron.* all things (U2)

evil *adj.* very bad, wicked (S3)

excerpt *n.* a short text taken from a longer one (U2)

excursion *n.* a short journey arranged so that a group of people can visit a place (U3)

to expect *v.* to demand, to want (U9)

F

to face your fears *v.* to confront things you are scared of (U1)

fan *n.* enthusiastic admirer (U8)

faster *adv.* more rapidly (U8)

fight *n.* a situation in which two people or groups hurt each other (U3)

fire extinguisher *n.* a metal container with water or chemicals in it, used for stopping small fires (U7)

fitness *n.* ability to run or do physical work for a long time (U8)

fizzy *adj.* releasing little bubbles (U2)

flood *n.* a very large amount of water that covers an area that is usually dry (U7)

to flow *v.* to move along in a steady way, like water (U9)

front page *n.* first page (U10)

fundraising *adj.* collecting money for a specific purpose (U8)

G

garbage *n.* waste material, such as paper, empty containers and food thrown away (U3)

to go along with *v.* to agree with (U1)

to go over the edge *v.* to go too far (U1)

to ground *v.* to make someone stay at home as a punishment (U5)

H

to hang around with *v.* to spend time with (U1)

happiest *adj.* that gives you the most pleasure (U2)

harvest *n.* when grain, vegetables, etc. are collected from the fields (U4)

healthy *adj.* good for your body (U3)

to hit the slopes *v.* to go skiing or snowboarding (U1)

to hook *v.* to attract and keep (U10)

I

I don't mind *idiom* it's not important to me (U1)

to ignore *v.* not to pay attention to someone (S4)

illegal *adj.* against the law (S1)

item *n.* a single article, especially one article in a list (U7)

J

jewellery *n.* things that you wear for decoration, such as rings and necklaces (U6)

job *n.* a task (U5)

joke *n.* something that you say or do to make people laugh (S4)

K

keyboard *n.* all the keys on a computer that you press to make it work (U6)

kind *n.* type (U3)

kind *adj.* saying or doing things that show that you want to make someone happy (S4)

kit *n.* a set of tools, equipment etc. for a particular purpose (U7)

kitchen *n.* the room where you cook and prepare food (U7)

L

laundry basket *n.* a container for clothes etc. that need to be washed (U6)

lazy *adj.* not liking to do work (S2)

leftovers *n.* things that remain (U6)

to listen *v.* to try to hear and understand sounds or what someone is saying (U5)

local *adj.* relating to the particular area you live in (U3)

to lock *v.* to close a door so that no one can enter (U5)

to loosen *v.* to relax (U1)

M

to make fun of *v.* to make unkind comments about someone (S4)

maybe *adv.* possibly (U5)

meal *n.* breakfast, lunch or dinner (U3)

mess *n.* a state of disorder (U3)

N

neighbour *n.* someone who lives next to you or near you (U5)

to never give up *v.* to continue, even in a difficult situation (S4)

noise *n.* an unpleasantly loud sound (U3)

O

opportunity *n.* a chance to do something (U3)

P

to pay off *v.* to have a good result (U10)

people *n.* men, women and children (U2)

pier *n.* a platform stretching into a river (U7)

to pitch *v.* to throw a ball to a batter (U8)

playground *n.* an area in which children can play (U3)

to please *v.* to make happy (S4)

to plunge *v.* to fall or move down quickly with a lot of force (U7)

power failure *n.* a period of time when there is no electricity supply (U7)

powerful *adj.* strong (U9)

to pretend *v.* to act as if something is true when it is not (U1)

to prevent *v.* to stop something from happening (U7)

produce *n.* food grown on a farm to be sold (U3)

R

ready *adj.* prepared (U7)

really *adv.* very (U10)

to relive *v.* to experience something that happened in past times (U2)

reluctant *adj.* slow and unwilling (U3)

to remember *v.* to call to mind (U7)

to be remembered *v.* to be famous for something important that you did in the past (U2)

Richter scale *n.* a system of numbers used for measuring how powerful an earthquake is (U7)

to run (the tap) *v.* to leave the tap open (U6)

S

saddest *adj.* that makes you most unhappy (U2)

safe *adj.* not likely to cause any physical injury or harm (U5)

scared *adj.* frightened (U2)

scavenger hunt *n.* a game in which people try to find different objects (U6)

to scrap *v.* to throw away (U6)

scream *n.* a shriek (S3)

to seem *v.* to appear (U5)

self-control *n.* ability to manage your actions and emotions (U8)

to sharpen *v.* to make pointed (U1)

shelf *n.* a board to put things on, fixed to a wall or in a closet (U6)

ship *n.* a large boat (U2)

to shock *v.* to surprise and upset (U10)

shocking *adj.* very upsetting (U7)

skating rink *n.* a place or building where you can skate (U3)

sleigh *n.* a vehicle for travelling on snow (U4)

smoke *n.* white, grey or black gas produced by something burning (U7)

to store *v.* to keep things until you need them (U7)

strange *adj.* unusual or surprising (S2)

street corner *n.* a place where roads meet (U3)

strength *n.* a positive quality (U9)

struggle *n.* a fight (U4)

stuck *adj.* unable to continue because something is too difficult (U9)

summer *n.* the season between spring and autumn (June, July, August in Canada) (U4)

supplies *n.* articles necessary for a particular purpose (U7)

to sweat *v.* to perspire (U1)

T

table tennis *n.* an indoor game played on a table by two or four players who hit a small plastic ball to each other across a net (U3)

to take apart *v.* to break into its components (U6)

to talk back *v.* to answer rudely (U5)

teenager *n.* someone from the age of 13 to 19, inclusive (U3)

to throw *v.* to send through the air with force (U8)

tile *n.* a square piece of hard material that is used for covering roofs, walls or floors (U6)

time capsule *n.* a container that is filled with objects from a particular time, to give people in the future an idea of what life was like then (U2)

together *adv.* with each other (U3)

traffic *n.* the vehicles moving along a street (U7)

trash *n.* garbage, rubbish

trick *n.* something that deceives somebody (S3)

truth or dare *n.* a game where you choose to answer a question correctly or do what someone tells you to do (U1)

tummy *n.* child's word for stomach (U2)

to turn out *v.* to have a particular result (U10)

to turn up *v.* to happen (U1)

U

underground *adj.* under the earth's surface (U2)

to understand *v.* to comprehend (U5)

V

to vanish *v.* to disappear (S1)

W

to wake someone up *v.* to make someone stop sleeping (U5)

to warn *v.* to tell someone that something bad or dangerous may happen, so that she or he can avoid it or prevent it (S1)

waste *n.* material which has been made useless (U6)

to waste *v.* to use more than necessary (U6)

weakness *n.* a negative quality (U9)

to welcome *v.* to greet (U4)

whispery *adj.* very quiet (S3)

wild *adj.* out of control (U5)

to win *v.* to come first (U8)

winter *n.* the season between autumn and spring (December, January, February in Canada) (U4)

to work out *v.* to do physical exercises (U1)

to worry *v.* to be anxious (U9)

Y

younger *adj.* not as old as you are now (U2)

youth *n.* a teenager (U3)